That Way and No Other

That Way and No Other

Following God through Storm and Drought

Amy Carmichael

Edited by Carolyn Kurtz

PLOUGH PUBLISHING HOUSE

Published by Plough Publishing House
Walden, New York
Robertsbridge, England
Elsmore, Australia
www.plough.com

Plough produces books, a quarterly magazine, and Plough.com to encourage people and help them put their faith into action. We believe Jesus can transform the world and that his teachings and example apply to all aspects of life. At the same time, we seek common ground with all people regardless of their creed.

Plough is the publishing house of the Bruderhof, an international Christian community. The Bruderhof is a fellowship of families and singles practicing radical discipleship in the spirit of the first church in Jerusalem (Acts 2 and 4). Members devote their entire lives to serving God, one another, and their neighbors. They renounce private property and share everything. To learn more about the Bruderhof's faith, history, and daily life, see Bruderhof.com. (Views expressed by Plough authors are their own and do not necessarily reflect the position of the Bruderhof.)

Cover art copyright © 2020 by Julie Lonneman. Photograph of Amy Carmichael from Wikimedia Commons (public domain).
All quotes from books by Amy Carmichael are copyright by The Dohnavur Fellowship and reprinted here by permission. All rights reserved. This edition is published by special arrangement with CLC Ministries International, Fort Washington, Pennsylvania, USA.

A catalog record for this book is available from the British Library.
Library of Congress Cataloging-in-Publication Data
Names: Carmichael, Amy, 1867-1951 author. | Kurtz, Carolyn, editor.
Title: That way and no other : following God through storm and drought / Amy Carmichael ; edited by Carolyn Kurtz.
Description: 1st edition. | Walden, New York : Plough Publishing House, 2020. | Series: Plough spiritual guides: backpack classics
Identifiers: LCCN 2019056968 (print) | LCCN 2019056969 (ebook) | ISBN 9780874863031 (paperback) | ISBN 9780874863055 (ebook)
Subjects: LCSH: Spiritual life--Christianity. | Carmichael, Amy, 1867-1951. | Missionaries--India--Biography. | Missionaries--Ireland--Biography. | Church work with children--India. | Dohnavur Fellowship--History.
Classification: LCC BV4501.3 .C26 2020 (print) | LCC BV4501.3 (ebook) | DDC 248.4--dc23
LC record available at https://lccn.loc.gov/2019056968
LC ebook record available at https://lccn.loc.gov/2019056969

Printed in the United States of America

Contents

Who Was Amy Carmichael?

Carolyn Kurtz

THE SUN HAD BARELY RISEN when Amy Carmichael heard someone outside the bungalow to which she'd returned in the night after a year's absence. Stepping to the door, she saw a tense-looking woman with a small girl at her side. Amy invited them in.

Glancing around, the woman quickly explained that seven-year-old Preena had turned up the previous evening, having escaped a nearby Hindu shrine. Although she'd sheltered this unknown child overnight, she said, "I would not have dared keep her an hour longer. If you had not been here, I would have returned her to the temple." Pushing the girl toward Amy, the woman hurried away.

The child instinctively sensed that finding Amy Carmichael was a turning point. Fifty years later Preena recalled, "The first thing she did was to put me on her lap and kiss me. . . . From that day she became my mother, body and soul." Amy, however, did not immediately grasp the moment's significance; she did not realize she had just found her life's vocation.

For four years, with a married British missionary couple, the Walkers, Amy had travelled by bullock cart throughout Tirunelveli and Travancore, in what are now the southern Indian states of Tamil Nadu and Kerala. Four young Indian women had joined them. The group would camp several weeks at some chosen spot, making evangelistic excursions to surrounding villages. It was during one such mission in March 1901 that they stopped at Pannaivilai, just in time for Preena to find them there.

The seven-year-old told Amy she'd run away before, sensing that temple dances led to something ugly. She had found her home, twenty miles distant, in three days. But temple women had tracked her down, and her mother, fearing divine vengeance, had handed her over. Back inside guarded temple walls, the women had punished Preena with hot iron brands. Now she stated she would stay with Amy forever.

Mr. Walker made inquiries in the village to verify the child's story, and soon several women identifying themselves as servants of the gods arrived at Pannaivilai to reclaim her. A crowd gathered, but when Preena refused to go with them the people dispersed.

Preena began telling her new mother what went on in the temple – "things that darkened the sunlight," wrote Amy. "It was impossible to forget those things. Wherever we went after that day we were constrained to gather facts about what appeared a great secret traffic in the souls and bodies of young children."

Amy and one of her Indian comrades camped at the edge of a temple village to glean information. With her dark hair and eyes, Amy had only to darken her skin with coffee to pass as Indian when she and Ponnammal mingled with an evening throng of pilgrims. "We discovered nothing by asking questions. To ask was to close every door. We learned by quietly sharing as much as we could in the life of the people, by listening, not by questioning." They found what Amy described as a fine net thrown over the land. "And the net is alive: it can feel and it can hold."

The two learned that poverty or shame could drive a young mother – or a widow with no hope of finding her daughter a husband – to sell her child to a temple. Or parents might offer an infant in exchange for spiritual merit. Once "wedded to the gods," little girls were trained in temple chores and elaborate dances. But they also became sexual slaves to serve the lusts of priests and worshippers.

To explain the complexities of Hinduism, Amy quoted Sir Monier Williams: "It has its highly spiritual and abstract side, suited to the metaphysical philosopher; its practical and concrete side, suited to the man of affairs and the man of the world; its aesthetic and ceremonial side, suited to the man of poetic feeling and imagination." Yet it also included "the most grotesque forms of idolatry and the most degrading varieties of superstition."

Amy wrote to supporters in England, hinting at the sexual abuse disguised as religion, but her reports were rebuffed as exaggeration. She felt desperate. "The thing that we wanted to do appeared to be impossible. It was all disappointment, and never a little one saved."

"At last a day came when the burden grew too heavy for me; and then it was as though the tamarind trees about the house were not tamarind, but olive, and under one of those trees our Lord Jesus knelt, and he knelt alone. And I knew that this was his burden, not mine.

It was he who was asking me to share it with him, not I who was asking him to share it with me."

AMY WAS BORN in Ireland on December 16, 1867, the first child of Catherine and David Carmichael, whose family owned the mills in the coastal village of Millisle. "Blueness of sea that looked happy, grayness of sea that looked anxious, greenness of sea that looked angry – these are my first memories of color," Amy would write.

A Christian revival that swept the region in 1859 affected Catherine and David, and by extension their children. Amy's earliest memory was that "after the nursery light had been turned low and I was quite alone, I used to smooth a little place on the sheet, and say aloud, but softly, to our Father, 'Please come and sit with me.'" It was at bedtime, too, that she absorbed songs and stories. When her mother said one night that Jesus answers prayer, inspiration struck three-year-old Amy: before falling asleep, she prayed for her brown eyes to turn blue. Next morning, she eagerly mounted a chair before the mirror – and was astounded by brown eyes staring back. She ran to report the unanswered request. Perhaps her mother said the sensible words, or else they simply spoke themselves in her mind: "Isn't no an answer?"

Young Amy could be stubborn. "The will of a child can be like steel," she reminisced of an occasion when she refused to deliver soup to poor neighbors. "My mother did not know what to do with me, for I would not give in, and was not at all sorry." As Mrs. Carmichael prepared to take the soup, Amy glimpsed her "reflected in the mirror. And then I found myself looking not at her hands tying on her bonnet, but at her face. Suddenly something melted inside me. In one moment I was in her arms."

Catherine passed on to her children a love for all living things. Like her, Amy hated cruelty, and her first memory of feeling fury was on seeing another child torment a frog.

Naturally, lively interaction with four brothers and two sisters formed Amy's character. One evening the returning Carmichael parents were horrified by the sight of Amy leading two brothers along the edge of the roof. Another time she and the same brothers took a rowboat onto Strangford Lough, where tides are said to be among the strongest in the world. Amy steered while the other two rowed, but when the seaward current grabbed the boat, their efforts were powerless. "Sing!" the boys commanded. Amy's song caught the attention of the coast guard, who sped to the children's rescue.

Amy's escapades continued after she was sent to a Yorkshire boarding school at age twelve, and she was often in trouble. Yet it was here that she experienced her conversion, one day during silence in chapel. Although she had always trusted Jesus' love, resting in it as in her mother's arms, "I had not understood that there was something more to do, something that may be called coming to him, or opening the door to him, or giving oneself to him," she said later. "During those quiet few minutes, in his great mercy the Good Shepherd answered the prayers of my mother and father . . . and drew me, even me, into his fold."

Around this time financial difficulties hit the Carmichael mills, and Amy was called home from school. Then on April 12, 1885, David Carmichael died of pneumonia. He was fifty-four.

Amy, now seventeen, supported her mother by homeschooling the youngest children. One of her sisters recalled, "If anybody asked me what were the strongest impressions Amy made on me in her youth, I think I would say – her enthusiasms. She would kindle so quickly to anything that promised the betterment of the poor or unhappy. She was fired by the hope that socialism presented when she first read about it."

One Sunday the Carmichaels passed a shabbily dressed woman on the street, weighed down with bundles. "We had never seen such a thing in Presbyterian Belfast," Amy said later. On impulse, she and her brothers turned to help the woman. But when other churchgoers passed by, Amy "felt crimson" with embarrassment. Just then, words from First Corinthians "flashed as it were through the gray drizzle: 'Gold, silver, precious stones, wood, hay, stubble . . . the fire shall try every man's work.' I knew something had happened that had changed life's values. Nothing could ever matter again but the things that were eternal."

Amy started gathering local children in her family's home on Sunday afternoons; and in 1888 she oversaw construction of a metal hall for outreach to Belfast mill girls. With no money for the project, she prayed – and funds came. Trusting God's provision became her norm. The hall, seating five hundred, opened in January 1889 and is still in use 130 years later. Amy dubbed it The Welcome, although privately she called it the "tin tabernacle."

Starting in 1888, Amy attended several Keswick Conventions. Founded in 1875, the organization's purpose was to deepen spiritual life, and Amy met sincere Christians at the yearly conference, including evangelist Dwight L. Moody, Hudson Taylor of the China Inland Mission, and Quaker Robert Wilson, a Keswick Convention founder now in his sixties, who soon became a close friend of the Carmichael family.

At age twenty-one, Amy moved to England, joining a mission to Manchester factory workers. She took a room in the slum, but her health suffered, and Wilson invited her to join his household in Keswick. She assumed she would support him the rest of his life. However on January 13, 1892, she distinctly heard the words, "Go ye," which she understood as a call to overseas mission.

During the following months, as she regained her health, Amy studied the Bible and discussed mission with Wilson. "Thee must never say, thee must never even let thyself think, 'I have won that soul for Christ,'" he told her one day, stopping the carriage by a slate quarry. "There was one who asked a stonebreaker at work by the roadside, 'Friend, which blow broke the stone?' And the stonebreaker answered, 'The first one, and the last one, and every one between.'" Recalling his story years later, Amy added, "The joy of the winner and helper of souls is something apart from every other joy, but it is tarnished the moment the *I* comes in."

Eight months after hearing the call to foreign missionary work, Amy moved to London for training at China Inland Mission headquarters. The organization's doctor ruled that her health was too poor for the conditions in China, so in March 1893 she sailed for an outpost in Japan instead. Her fifteen-month sojourn there taught her some valuable lessons, such as the importance of wearing local dress. She would never forget the challenge of a Japanese man who asked her to show him Jesus' way of life *being lived*.

Excruciating headaches forced her to leave in 1894 and she returned to Britain. Then a letter invited her to India. In October 1895, twenty-seven-year-old Amy set sail once more, this time for good. She would never see Britain or Ireland again. When she died in January 1951, at eighty-three, she had spent more than fifty-five years in her adopted country.

AFTER PREENA'S UNEXPECTED ARRIVAL, Amy continued to evangelize. Nicknamed "Elf," Preena held a special place in Amy's heart: "As evening by evening we returned from work, there was a child's loving welcome, little loving arms were round one's neck. I remember wakening up to the knowledge that there had been a very empty corner somewhere in me that the work had never filled."

The missionaries' base was Dohnavur, a rather desolate village established by Europeans seventy years earlier. The Walkers chose the cottages and bungalow, and the group settled into this compound, encircled by a low mud wall and "haunted by flocks of noisy goats," according to Amy. She was better impressed by the view. "Framed between red roofs and foliage, there are far blue glimpses of mountains . . . scarped with bare crags, which in the early morning are sometimes pink, and in the evening, purple. But the time to see the mountains in their glory is when the southwest monsoon is flinging its masses of cloud across to us. Then the mountains, waking from the lazy sleep of the long, hot months, catch the clouds on their pointed fangs, toss them back and harry them, wrap themselves up in robes of them, and go to sleep again."

At Dohnavur, more little girls began arriving. In March 1904, an Indian pastor brought thirteen-day-old Amethyst – a special victory, as her mother had been about to sell her to a shrine. It was a shock when the little one died soon after. Amy later learned that young widows were often mistreated. Amethyst had been born after her father's death.

By June there were seventeen young girls in Dohnavur. But during the next half year, two more infants died. After an epidemic took the last of these, Amy wrote:

When we went back to the empty nursery, and folded up the baby's little things and put them away, we felt as if we could not begin all over again. But we were shown that what we had been through was only meant to make us the more earnestly persist. So we set apart the sixth of each month, the date of our little Indraneela's passing, as a prayer day for the temple children, that they may be found and redeemed from temple service; and for ourselves that we may love them according to the love of the Lord. Sometimes in faraway places, upon that very day God has signally worked for the deliverance of a little one in danger, and always he has met us and renewed our strength. We have never had another Indraneela, but our empty nursery has been filled to overflowing.

When Amy realized her growing family needed a full-time mother, she struggled to reconcile homemaking with her missionary calling. "Could it be right to turn from so much that might be of profit . . . and become just nursemaids?" Then to her mind sprang a picture of Jesus washing his disciples' feet. "He took a towel – the Lord of Glory did that," she wrote. "Is it the bondservant's business to say which work is large and which is small, which unimportant and which worth doing? The question answered itself, and was not asked again."

And so Amy – now "Amma" to a houseful of daughters – experienced all the joys and anxieties of motherhood that she had thought would never be hers. To a Tamil proverb, "Children tie the mother's feet," she added, "we let our feet be tied for love of Him whose feet were pierced."

After Amy's decision to devote herself to the children, many more came. As keenly as the three deaths had been grieved, every arrival was celebrated. And since birthdates were rarely known, "coming days" were acknowledged each year. In 1906 the family grew to seventy, and by 1913 that number had doubled.

"With the coming of each new child we learned a little more of the private ways of this dreadful underworld of India," Amy wrote. "Sometimes we felt as though the things that we had seen and heard had killed forever the laughter in us. But children must have laughter round about them. Some guests to Dohnavur see nothing but the laughter side, the joy of flowers and babies; but a few see deeper."

As more children were rescued, more housing was needed. The very day that Amy suggested brickmaking in Dohnavur, to build a fire- and termite-proof nursery, a gift of money arrived – the exact amount needed. The other pressing need was for consecrated women to care for the little girls. Finding such women was a challenge. In Amy's words, "The care of young children is not among the 'honorable' occupations of South India," and some early helpers left more quickly than they'd come. Such disappointments convinced Amy that the team needed a clear commitment "to unite and fortify them."

Ponnammal was among the first to join Amy. Mabel Wade, a Yorkshire nurse, came in 1907. By 1916 seven young Indian women, including Preena, had committed themselves. In March of that year they formed a Sisterhood of the Common Life, named for a fourteenth-century group of brothers who, according to Thomas à Kempis, "humbly imitated the manner of the apostolic life, and having one heart and mind in God, brought every man what was his own into the common stock." Love, born of dedication to God, was the cord that bound the Indian and British sisters.

Perhaps Dohnavur's "times of vital silence" stem from the Quaker worship of Amy's months with Robert

Wilson. Childhood memories of long Sunday sermons – when she'd devised tricks to combat boredom – played a role too, for she kept Dohnavur worship brief, commenting, "never forget that the human should not be drawn out like a piece of elastic and held so."

Uppermost for Amy was guiding her children and coworkers toward Christ. She recalled how lonely she'd been when first in India, after making her final break with home and family. When mail arrived from England one day, "she ran to her bedroom, locked the door, knelt by the bed, and – read the letters aloud, one by one, to her heavenly Father." Sharing the memory with a young Dohnavur sister, Amy said, "Treat him like that. Make him your chief love and friend."

Over time, Amy framed a "pattern" for the members of the fellowship:

My Vow. Whatsoever thou sayest unto me, by thy grace I will do it.

My Constraint. Thy love, O Christ, my Lord.

My Confidence. Thou art able to keep that which I have committed unto thee.

My Joy. To do thy will, O God.

My Discipline. That which I would not choose, but which thy love appoints.

My Prayer. Conform my will to thine.

My Motto. Love to live; live to love.

My Portion. The Lord is the portion of mine inheritance.

She described the blessings that flowed from allowing this pattern to shape one's life: "We were first shown the crystal quality of loyalty, for our prayer-life together was to become the chief thing with us all. And it meant depth of conviction about certain matters, and singleness of mind. . . . It meant peacefulness, too, and . . . a spontaneous gaiety."

Amy made "one careful rule: the absent must be safe with us. Criticism, therefore, was taboo." The team understood; they were not to gossip against each other. "Learn to be a deep well," Amy told her Dohnavur family. "A deep well doesn't talk." More than once, noticing tension between members, she stopped a prayer meeting until trust was restored.

IN 1911 Amy learned that temples took boys as well as girls; boys were also in moral danger in dramatic companies. Seven years later the first little boy arrived in Dohnavur. By 1926, seventy or eighty had come. Two British men joined the Fellowship and led the boys' home for twenty years. Indian men eventually joined as well.

Amy suffered much during her last twenty years. One night in October 1931 she fell into an open pit, and she never fully recovered from her injuries. In the end she rarely left her room. Yet that suffering bore rich fruit as she continued to guide her community. Fifteen books went to print during those years.

Looking back in 1937, Amy wrote, "When the fellowship was first formed many called it utopian to expect that as more joined us we could ever continue to be of one mind in a house. And yet we saw vital unity in our God's pattern for a fellowship of Christians. Would he have set an impossible pattern?" And thinking toward the future, she said, "When decisions have to be made, don't look back and wonder what I would have done. Look up, and light will come to do what our Lord and Master would have you do."

Dohnavur Fellowship cared for boys until 1984. It still makes a home for girls. Although dedicating children to temples for prostitution was outlawed as early as 1924, the practice persists in some parts of the country, as do the economic and social pressures that lead desperate families to give up their children. As in Amy's time, children at Dohnavur are raised to serve God through service to others. Many move on to higher education, marry, or find jobs. Some become Dohnavur coworkers. As of 2019, all members are Indian.

THE FOLLOWING TOPICALLY ARRANGED SELECTIONS from Amy Carmichael's writings are merely an introduction; they should inspire readers to read her books. She authored thirty-five, many of which are still in print. Her first, *From Sunrise Land* (letters from Japan), came out in 1895. *Things As They Are* (1903), *Overweights of Joy* (1906), *Beginning of a Story* (1908), *Lotus Buds* (1909), *Gold Cord* (1932), and *Though the Mountains Shake* (1943) chronicle the Dohnavur venture. Then there are biographies: *Walker of Tinnevelly* (1916) tells of the missionary who trained Amy in Tamil and introduced her to Indian ways; *Ponnammal* (1918), *Mimosa* (1924), *The Widow of the Jewels* (1928), *Ploughed Under* (1934), and *Kohila* (1939) are stories of Dohnavur sisters; *Ragland* (1922) is about an early British missionary; and *Raj* (1926) depicts an Indian Robin Hood with whom Amy had several encounters. *If* (1938) and *His Thoughts Said . . . His Father Said . . .* (1941) offer answers to questions about life issues. *Rose from Briar* (1933), *Gold by Moonlight* (1935), and *Windows* (1937) offer meditations on nature – or on uplifting quotes and Bible verses – for readers dealing with grief or pain. A book of poetry set to music, *Wings* (1960), and a book of excerpts from her letters, *Candles in the Dark* (1981), were published after her death.

The passages in this little book have been chosen to help guide readers in discerning their own call to follow Jesus, and to challenge and encourage them to remain true in the all-or-nothing way of discipleship that Amy modeled. Like any disciple, Amy experienced discouragement, animosity, betrayal, and failure – along with quiet, decisive victories. Her hard-earned insights and wisdom can strengthen believers in the battles we face today.

Carolyn Kurtz, a member of the Bruderhof community, has compiled and edited two other titles in this series: The Reckless Way of Love: Notes on Following Jesus, *by Dorothy Day, and* The Scandal of Redemption: When God Liberates the Poor, Saves Sinners, and Heals Nations, *by Oscar Romero.*

Reading Amy Carmichael Today

Katelyn Beaty

READING ABOUT THE HEROINES of Christian
missions, it's hard not to envy their sense of adventure.
There's Lottie Moon and her band of Baptist missionaries riding across China, on one trip visiting forty-four
villages in eleven days. There's Betsey Stockton, a freed
slave who attended classes at Princeton Theological
Seminary before sailing to Hawaii in 1823 to educate
children. Elizabeth "Betty" Greene is the evangelical
Amelia Earhart, a jungle pilot who co-founded Mission
Aviation Fellowship after serving in World War II. In
her biography, Greene recalls that she once was asked
to transport a certain Marine Corps general, who didn't
think women should fly planes, across Peru. After
Greene made a dead-stick landing on a stretch of the

Amazon River, the general seemed to feel differently about women pilots.

The story of modern missions is the story of adventurous women. They are remembered for their radical service to God, yes, but also for challenging conventions of womanhood, even while affirming traditional gender roles. Together, their biographies attest to a time when women, though often restricted in their own cultures, could travel the globe as evangelists and entrepreneurs. Global missions gave them a chance to preach, teach, and lead in ways they couldn't have back home.

By the late nineteenth century, more women than men were in the missions field. These women seem largely unhindered by Victorian ideals of separate spheres for men and women and the idealization of marriage and motherhood. To be sure, many of the missionaries were wives and mothers. But many others were prepared to forgo marriage and motherhood as well as home and homeland for the sake of their cause.

Such was the case for Amy Carmichael. Born into a devout Presbyterian family in Ireland, it seems she possessed a nascent calling to give her life to God. By age twenty, after the death of her father, she was caring for her younger siblings and for Belfast mill girls, who worked grueling hours in poor conditions with few protections. In response, Amy raised funds to build an outreach hall for the mill workers. Here and throughout her life, Amy's natural stubbornness and compassion combined to inspire acts of great service.

Amy's role models were men: Dwight L. Moody, Robert Wilson, and Hudson Taylor, the father of modern missions and founder of China Inland Mission. After hearing Taylor speak at a revivalist Keswick Convention in 1887, Amy heard God say, "Go ye." She understood that, despite her physical weakness owing to neuralgia, she would follow in Taylor's footsteps. After a brief stint in Japan, she landed in India, the locus of her ministry. She never returned home.

DOHNAVUR, THE VILLAGE IN SOUTHERN INDIA where Amy Carmichael lived until her death in 1951, would soon become an oasis of children's laughter and verdant gardens. But along the way there were many obstacles to confront, both within and without. Amy faced loneliness, discouragement, and discord among her staff, in addition to the threat of disease and malnutrition, cultural barriers, and local animosity. Some locals accused her and the other missionaries of kidnapping children. Amy was convinced, however, that her greatest opposition was Satan, who wanted to keep Indian children trapped in the "darkness" of Hinduism.

What sounds like cultural imperialism to our ears takes on a new dimension when we learn the fate of many children dedicated to the service of Hindu gods. In the book *Lotus Buds,* Amy recounts a conversation with a medical missionary who says she heard "frightened cries, indignant cries, sometimes sharp cries as of pain" from the temple next door. After inquiring with police, who assure her that the children were "only" being beaten, the missionary realized that the children were being sexually abused.

But Amy also showed a shrewdness rare among missionaries operating in countries ruled by the British Empire. She saw that poor families turned to temple prostitution for economic and social security. One mother whose children participated in the rituals contrasted the glory of having her daughter dance before high-caste Hindus with "the groveling life of your Christians." The mother defended the temple practices as ancient custom, and said changing them would be arrogant. Here, we recall generations of Christian missions that led to so much cultural destruction done in the name of Jesus around the globe. But Amy found a way to honor India's beliefs and customs while opposing the abuse. "The thing we fight is not India or Indian, in essence of development," she writes. "It is something alien to the old life of the people. . . . It is like a parasite which has settled upon the bough of some noble forest tree – on it, but not of it." Today, development workers might recall Amy Carmichael's sensitivity while addressing female genital mutilation in Africa and the Middle East. Likewise, missionaries who hope to end polygamy in sub-Saharan Africa might address the underlying poverty that leads many women to seek economic security in a shared husband.

LIKE MANY WOMEN in the missions field, Amy Carmichael remained single for life. According to biographer Ruth Ann Tucker, she struggled early on with a fear of the future, and the possibility of lifelong loneliness. During her fifteen months in Japan, she went to be alone with God in a cave. "The devil kept on whispering, 'It is all right now, but what about afterwards? You are going to be very lonely.'" Amy prayed desperately, and God answered, "None of them that trust in me shall be desolate." If Amy struggled with singleness for the next fifty years, she does not mention it much in her writing. In fact, she might have wished for more time alone. As more children arrived at Dohnavur, Amy (now "Amma," or mother) struggled with the responsibilities of mothering and homemaking. In *Overweights of Joy,* she notes that a whole year has passed since she last wrote. "For we can only write in odd corners of time, and sometimes time does not seem to have any odd corners. Quiet is even rarer." By 1913, 140 children were in her care, and several English and Indian women had joined her in the work. By 1916, Amy Carmichael had established the Sisterhood of the Common Life, a Protestant order that imitated medieval communities of celibate men and women. The sisters were expected to remain single; if they intended to marry, they had to leave. Absent a husband and biological children, Amy nonetheless stitched together a family in the form of her rescued children and her sisters in the mission. At the time of Amy's death, the Dohnavur family numbered around nine hundred.

Many of Amy Carmichael's admirers – most notably Elisabeth Elliot, widow of slain missionary Jim Elliot – have seen in her an icon of submissive femininity in her whole-life surrender to God. In one of her popular essays on womanhood, Elliot writes that the essence of femininity is surrender: first, in the surrender of "her independence, her name, her destiny, her will, herself" in marriage vows and the marriage bed, and later in her bodily surrender to welcoming new life in her womb. "Perhaps the exceptional women in history have been given a special gift – a charism – because they made themselves nothing," writes Elliot, who goes on to compare Amy Carmichael to Mary the mother of Jesus.

Indeed, Amy Carmichael's books repeat the theme of sometimes painful surrender to the will of God, a constant battle between self-will and submission to a higher calling. Yet we would be mistaken to only see in her missions a lesson in acquiescence. Her life's work is nothing if not an expression of determination, grit, and leadership – attributes that Elliot and others would very well call masculine. Dohnavur grew as it did precisely because she had initiated and led a campaign to rescue children from the world of temple prostitution. According to scholar Nancy Jiwon Cho, Amy Carmichael developed in her extensive writing a "particular theology" that displays "hope for the development of an authentic Indian Christianity that responds to the experiences and needs of Indians" – a theology that would inspire subsequent generations of Christian women and men alike. If men are like Christ in their role as initiator, protector, and provider, it's hard not to see in Amy Carmichael an expression of such Christ-like masculinity: in initiating rescue efforts, protecting the most vulnerable, and providing a home and spiritual comfort for hundreds of people. Then again, the self-surrender that Amy Carmichael writes about is also the surrender of Christ to the will of his Father. Thus, Amy Carmichael provides not so much a lesson in feminine submission as in Christian submission. There is no biblical call to take up one's masculine or feminine cross – only to surrender all to the will of God.

By the time of Amy Carmichael's death in 1951, women's global missions had started to lag. According to journalist Wendy Murray, the modernist–fundamentalist controversies earlier in the century, coupled with postwar prosperity and the baby boom, had circumscribed women's roles to the home. The mainstream feminist backlash to these narrower roles spurred its own conservative Christian backlash – what Ruth Ann Tucker has called a "neofundamentalism" that arguably continues to this day. Major missions organizations such as the Southern Baptist International Mission Board have in recent decades emphasized "proclamation ministries" such as direct evangelism and church planting – activities these organizations still reserve for men. Consequently, the number of women joining such missionary efforts has dwindled. American evangelicalism arguably remains in a neofundamentalist mode as a reaction to radically shifting gender norms in the culture at large. If she lived today, would Amy Carmichael be free to be Amy Carmichael?

Nevertheless, Amy Carmichael's life testifies that God raises up women in all times and places to take the gospel to the literal ends of the earth. Priscilla joined her husband to spread the good news in Rome, Greece, and Asia Minor in a time when women were largely seen as property and unfit for education. The aforementioned Betsey Stockton received seminary education as a freed slave, her very presence in a university classroom a testament against the racism woven into US law and custom. Amy Carmichael stepped aboard boats and trains to make her home halfway around the world, in a remote Indian village, to preach good news for the poor and freedom for the captives.

MANY YOUNG PEOPLE DREAM of embarking on such an adventure, to rescue trafficking victims, lift people in developing countries out of poverty, or otherwise "change the world." But Amy Carmichael's intrepid spirit and daring exploits are not the only reason her words still resonate a century later. Her thoughts in the pages that follow show a struggle common to every person who sets out to follow Jesus – the greatest adventure of all. In founding and guiding a community of women committed to providing a home for children, she learned what it takes for an individual to remain on such a demanding path, and what it takes to hold such a community together. The insights she imparts in dozens of books – many written during long years of convalescence and contemplation after a crippling accident – though specific to her time and place, are not just for women called to missionary work. Whatever the way we each might be called to serve God and humanity, Amy Carmichael's words in this little book can be a guiding light through the times of storm and drought that we will surely face.

Katelyn Beaty is the author of A Woman's Place: A Christian Vision for Your Calling in the Office, the Home, and the World *(Simon & Schuster) and serves as acquisitions editor for Brazos Press, a division of Baker Books. She lives in Brooklyn.*

I

Nothing Kept Back

DON'T SAY "IT DOESN'T MATTER" about anything (except your own feelings), for everything matters. Everything is important, even the tiniest thing. If you do everything, whether great or small, for the sake of your Savior and Lord, then you will be ready for whatever work he has chosen for you to do later.

IF THE NEXT STEP IS CLEAR, then the one thing to do is to take it. Don't pledge your Lord or yourself about the steps beyond. You don't see them yet.

BUT THE TIME FOR CHOICE is passing, and the chance to choose comes only once. I have often sat on the rocks by our mountain river and known that never for one moment was I looking at the water of a moment before.

OFTEN HIS CALL IS TO FOLLOW in paths we would not have chosen. But if in truth we say, "Anywhere, Lord," he takes us at our word and orders our goings, and then he puts a new song in our mouths, even a thanksgiving unto our God (Ps. 40:2–3). There is wonderful joy to be had from knowing that we are not in the way of our own choice. At least I have found it so. It gives a peculiar sort of confidence that even we – we who are nothings – are being "ordered" in our goings. It is very good to be "ordered" by our beloved Lord.

WE WALK ON ROCK, not on quicksand, when we obey. But there is no promise that the rock will be a leveled path, or like the carpet of roses that Cleopatra spread for the officers of Mark Antony.

Sooner or later God meets every trusting child who is following him up the mountain and says, "Now prove that you believe this that you have told me you believe, and that you have taught others to believe." Then is your opportunity. God knows, and you know, that there was always a hope in your heart that a certain way would not be yours. "Anything but that, Lord," had been your earnest prayer. And then, perhaps quite suddenly, you found your feet set on that way, that and no other. Do you still hold fast to your faith that he maketh your way perfect?

It does not look perfect. It looks like a road that has lost its sense of direction; a broken road, a wandering road, a strange mistake. And yet, either it is perfect, or all that you have believed crumbles like a rope of sand in your hands. There is no middle choice between faith and despair.

DON'T BE SURPRISED if temptations come. The one way is to throw yourself, everything you have to give, into the service to which you have been called. Paul spoke of himself as an offering poured out on "the sacrifice and service of your faith" (Phil. 2:17). That's what you must be, nothing kept back. And as you give all, you find all.

OUR LORD DID NOT SAY, "Go ye into all the world if you feel an ardent flame of love to all the people in it." He just said, "Go ye," and as we obey, he gives us all we need to lead them to him. And of course as we most of all need love, he gives it to us.

I THINK OFTEN WE ACCEPT the cross in theory, but when it comes to practice, we either do not recognize it for what it is, or we recognize it and try to avoid it. This we can always do, for the cross is something that can be taken up or left, just as we choose. It is *not* illness (that comes to all), or bereavement (that also is the common lot of man). It is something *voluntarily* suffered for the sake of the Lord Jesus, some denial of self that would not be if we were not following him.

THE STORY OF MARY breaking her pot of ointment (John 12:3) made me think of some among us who love their Savior and yet have not broken theirs. Something is held back, and so there is no outpouring of that love, no fragrance in the house. It is shut up, not given.

The days are passing so quickly. Soon it will be too late to pour all we have on his feet.

SOME FIND THEMSELVES in the midst of clouds and darkness because of the sinful deeds of others. And yet the wrongdoing of another should have no power to darken the way of a child of God. . . . The same word is comfort if the trouble be the result of our own doing. A wrong turning was taken at the foot of the hill. A wrong decision was made which has affected the whole course of life. The husband has been handicapped by a wife who can never enter into his deepest thoughts. The wife has been held from the highest she knew by the husband whose eyes were on the plains. Divided counsels in the bringing up of children tell upon the children. That means sorrow.

These circumstances were not the choice of God for those lives, but it is impossible to go back and begin again, and each day will bring its trials of patience and its private griefs.

View all this as a glorious chance to prove the power of your God to keep you in peace and in hope and in sweetness of spirit. In that sense "expose yourself" to those circumstances. Do not fret against them. Do not fret those who cause them to be by a dour countenance. *"Beloved, let us love"* is a wonderful word for such difficult situations. And love is happy, not dour.

BUT HE THAT IS DOWN need fear no fall. He that is down cannot get between God and his glory. And we knew then that there was nothing that he could not do through us if only we were nothing.

A CRUCIFIED LIFE cannot be self-assertive. It cannot protect itself. It cannot be startled into resentful words. The cup that is full of sweetness cannot spill bitter drops however sharply knocked.

I HAVE BEEN ASKING that our dearest Lord may have the joy (surely it must be a joy to him) of saying about each one of us, and about us all as a little company of his children: "I can count on him, on her, on them for *anything*. I can count on them for peace under any disappointment or series of disappointments, under any strain. I can trust them never to set limits, saying, 'Thus far, and no farther.' I can trust them not to offer the reluctant obedience of a doubtful faith, but to be as glad and merry as it is possible."

WE HAVE HAD FREQUENT JOY in the conversion of workmen during the last few years; most have been won not so much by what was said, as by what they saw in the everyday lives of the brothers, Indian or European, with whom they had to do. After they had seen something that they recognized as genuine and not of earth, they were willing to listen to the heavenly message, and then the entrance of our Savior's words brought light. "What made me want to be a Christian was seeing D.'s life. He never passed bad work, but he never lost his temper," said one in answer to a question about how he first became interested. D. came to us some years ago – a very thirsty and very unhappy boy. His thirst was quenched, his soul revived, and now the men he oversees bear this witness.

OUR MASTER HAS NEVER PROMISED us success. He demands obedience. He expects faithfulness. Results are his concern, not ours. And our reputation is a matter of no consequence at all.

ONE DAY I FELT the "I" in me rising hotly, and quite clearly – so clearly that I could show you the place on the floor of the room where I was standing when I heard it – the word came, "See in it a chance to die." To this day that word is life and release to me, and it has been to many others. See in this which seems to stir up all you most wish were *not* stirred up – see in it a chance to die to self in every form.

IN THE MOUNTAIN FORESTS to the west of Dohnavur our children find the cocoon of the atlas moth. It hangs from a twig, like a small brown bag tied up and left there and forgotten, a mere two inches of papery bag, and however often we see it we are never prepared for the miracle that emerges. For miracle it is: a large, almost bird-like creature struggles slowly through the very narrow neck of the bag. It has wings of crimson and pink, and blended green of various soft tones, shading off into terra cotta, brown, old-gold. Each wing has a window made of a clear substance like a delicate flake of talc, and on the edge of each is a pattern of wavy lines or dots, or some other dainty device. From wing-tip to wing-tip, nine, sometimes ten, inches of beauty, one of God's lovely wonders – that is what comes out of the brown paper bag. Nothing preserved in a glass case can show it, for the colors fade, but fresh from the hands of its Creator it is like something seen in a dream, pure faerie.

The radiant emergence of butterfly from chrysalis has often been used to illustrate that which will be when we put on immortality, but I am thinking of this exquisite thing in another way now. What if our life within these detaining months or years be like the life within the dull brown bag of the cocoon? One day something will emerge to the glory of his grace. Can we not, then, sustained by the bread of heaven and the good wine, continue in this hidden labor and spiritual fight till the sunset colors kindle and the stars appear?

2

Always a Soldier

LIFE IS A JOURNEY; it is a climb; it is also and always a war. The soldier of the Lord of Hosts is always a soldier. He dare not drivel down to any other kind of life.

WE CAN'T BE ENTANGLED in the affairs of this life if we are to be real soldiers. By its affairs I mean its chatter and its ways of thinking and deciding questions, its whole aspect and trend.

WHAT DO WE KNOW of travail? Of tears that scald before they fall? Of heartbreak? Of being scorned? God

Plough Quarterly FREE TRIAL ISSUE

Thank you for your purchase. If you liked this book, you'll want to try our magazine as well. Plough Quarterly brings together a diverse community of readers serious about putting their faith into action. And since you bought one of our books, we'd like to offer one issue free.

Give it a try! Just drop this completed card in the mail, and we'll send you a free trial issue. No cost, no obligation. If you like it, you'll get four more issues for just $18 (£14, €16). If you decide not to subscribe, simply write "cancel" on the invoice, return it, and owe nothing. Either way, the trial issue is yours to keep.

Name

Address

City   State   Zip

Email (We will not share your email address with any third party)   B20BK

Please allow 4–6 weeks for delivery of your free issue. No need to send money now; we will bill you later.

Plough Quarterly is $40 per year by single copy so you save 55%.

www.plough.com/trial

forgive us our love of ease. God forgive us that so often we turn our faces from a life that is even remotely like his. Forgive us that we all but worship comfort, the delight of the presence of loved ones, possessions, treasure on earth.

IN EVERY SPIRITUAL WORK for God there is need for one, several, or many (according to the size of the work) to be continually on the alert to detect the approach of the enemy of souls. . . .

The watcher learns many things as he is taught to watch. He learns never to be tired of loving, never to be shocked or startled out of his peace in Christ, never to be astonished by anything the devil does, never for one moment to forget that though he may be baffled, his Captain is not and never can be.

I HAVE NOTICED that often the first thing attacked is peace. (I suppose in earthly war the sentinel is likely to be the first to be put out of action if possible, and peace is our sentinel.) When our peace is shattered, vital prayer ceases, and the love which was to burn and not be put out – the love that finds sheer joy in sacrifice – fails utterly. So let us guard our peace. In disturbed times we can learn that circumstances have no power whatever over peace: "When he giveth quietness, who then (what then) can make trouble?" (Job 34:29).

IT IS THE LITTLE THINGS of life, the minute, unimportant-looking things, that are most likely to shatter our peace, because they are so small that we are very likely to fight them ourselves instead of looking up at once to our strong God.

DON'T BE SURPRISED if there is attack on your work, on *you* who are called to do it, on your innermost nature. . . . It must be so. The great thing is not to be surprised, not to count it strange – for that plays into the hand of the enemy.

Is it possible that anyone should set himself to exalt our beloved Lord and *not* become instantly a target for many arrows? The very fact that your work depends utterly on him and can't be done for a moment without him calls for a very close walk and a constant communion of spirit. This alone is enough to account for anything the enemy can do.

ALL THE GREAT STAINING TEMPTATIONS – to
selfishness, ambition, and other strong sins that violently
affront the soul – appear first in the region of the mind,
and can be fought and conquered there. We have been
given the power to close the door of the mind. We can
lose this power through disuse or increase it by use, by
the daily discipline of the inner man in things which
seem small, and by reliance upon the word of the spirit of
truth. "It is God which worketh in you both to will and
to do of his good pleasure" (Phil. 2:13). It is as though he
said, "Learn to live in your will, not in your feelings. Will
to banish that evil thing, that thought, that imagination,
and I will then will in you to perform that which you
most desire. Show that hateful visitor the door and I will
shut and bar it upon him; he will never reach as far as the
citadel of your being; your spirit shall not be defiled."

Speaking with the utmost simplicity, I would say this
means, "Do not fight the thing in detail: turn from it.
Do not look at it at all, or at yourself, but only at your
Lord." Satan was vanquished by Christ on the cross; he
need never conquer us. . . . Sing; "singing to yourselves"
is a word of divine wisdom (Eph. 5:19). Read; drive
your thoughts into a new channel till they run there of

themselves. Work; go and help lame dogs over stiles. Resolutely do something for someone else; and as you do this in dependence on him who is the rightful Master of your house, the unwelcome visitor will vanish. The attempt of the evil one to destroy you will react upon himself, perhaps by weakening his grip on another soul, perhaps by furnishing you with the key to the confidence of one who needs your help – for all the deeper experiences of sorrow and comfort, temptation and victory, sooner or later turn to keys. You will not only conquer, you will be more than conqueror through him who loved you (Rom. 8:37).

IT IS THE ETERNAL in books that makes them our friends and teachers – the paragraphs, the verses, that grip memory and ring down the years like bells, or call like bugles, or sound like trumpets; words of vision that open to us undying things and fix our eyes on them. We are not here, they tell us, for trivial purposes. . . . We are not here to be overcome, but to rise unvanquished after every knock-out blow, and laugh the laugh of faith, not fear.

TRUE CONVERSION does not mean peace, but a sword, and that sword can cut to the quick (Matt. 10:34). Only those who have gone through this severance with a loving, sensitive Indian brother or sister can even begin to imagine what confession in baptism costs. There is nothing in literature that shows it except our Lord's own words. It passes man's. So there is nothing careless in the joy of these baptism days, and yet joy triumphs. Again and again we have seen the Lord of Life victorious in the place where his foe is most strongly entrenched, and the wide waters under the mountains, and the little shining ford have seen – can we doubt it? – companies of angels rejoicing with him and with us, as we stood, sometimes in a rich flood of sunset color when his glory covered the heavens and the earth was full of his praise.

SUDDENLY THERE WAS a tumultuous rush of every produceable sound; tom-tom, conch shell, cymbal, flute, stringed instruments, and bells burst into chorus together. The idol was going to be carried out from his innermost shrine behind the lights; and as the great doors moved slowly, the excitement became intense, the thrill of it quivered through all the hall and sent a tremor through the crowd out to the street. But we passed out and away, and turned into a quiet courtyard known to us and talked to the women there.

There were three, one the grandmother of the house, one her daughter, and another a friend. The grandmother and her daughter were temple women. The eldest grandchild had been dedicated only a few months before. There were three more children: one Mungie, a lovable child of six, one a pretty three-year-old with a mop of beautiful curls, the youngest a baby just then asleep in its hammock; a little foot dangled out of the hammock, which was hung from a rafter in the verandah roof. We had come to talk to the grandmother and mother about the dear little six-year-old child, and hoped to find their heart.

But we seemed to talk to stone, hard as the stone of the temple tower that rose above the roofs, black against the purity of the moonlit sky. It was a bitter half hour. Some hours are like stabs to remember, or like the pitiless pressing down of an iron on living flesh. At last we could bear it no longer, and rose to go. As we left we heard the grandmother turn to her daughter's friend and say: "Though she heap gold on the floor as high as Mungie's neck, I would never let her go to those degraded Christians!"

Once again it was festival in the white light of the full moon, and once again we went to the same old Hindu town; for moonlight nights are times of opportunity, and the cool of evening brings strength for more than can be attempted in the heat of the day. And this time an adopted mother spoke words that ate like acid into steel as we listened.

Her adopted child is a slip of a girl, slim and light, with the ways of a shy thing of the woods. She made me think of a harebell growing all by itself in a rocky place, with stubbly grass about and a wide sky overhead. She was small and very sweet, and she slid onto my knee and whispered her lessons in my ear in the softest of little voices. She had gone to school for nearly a year, and liked to tell me all she knew.

"Do you go to school now?" I asked her.

She hung her head and did not answer.

"Don't you go?" I repeated.

She just breathed "No," and the little head dropped lower.

"Why not?" I whispered as softly.

The child hesitated. Some dim apprehension that the reason would not seem good to me troubled her, perhaps, for she would not answer. "Tell the Ammal, silly child!" said her foster mother, who was standing near. "Tell her you are learning to dance and sing and get ready for the gods!"

"I am learning to dance and sing and get ready for the gods," repeated the child obediently, lifting large, clear eyes to my face for a moment as if to read what was written there.

A group of men stood near us. I turned to them. "Is it right to give this little child to a life like that?" I asked them then.

They smiled a tolerant, kindly smile. "Certainly no one would call it right, but it is our custom," and they passed on. . . .

We had come to the town an hour or two earlier, and had seen, walking through the throng round the temple, two bright young girls in white. No girls of their age, except temple girls, would have been out at that hour of the evening, and we followed them home. They stopped when they reached the house where little Mungie lived, and then, turning, saw us and salaamed. One of the two was Mungie's elder sister. Little Mungie ran out to meet her sister, and, seeing us, eagerly asked for a book. So we stood in the open moonlight, and the little one tried to spell out the words of a text to show us she had not forgotten all she had learned, even though she, too, had been taken from school, and had to learn pages of poetry and the temple dances and songs.

The girls were jeweled and crowned with flowers, and they looked like flowers themselves; flowers in moonlight have a mystery about them not perceived in common day, but the mystery here was something wholly sorrowful. Everything about the children – they were hardly more than children – showed care and refinement of taste. There was no violent clash of color; the only vivid color note was the rich red of a silk underskirt that showed where the clinging folds of the white gold-embroidered sari were draped a little at the side. The effect was very dainty, and the girls' manners were modest and gentle. No one who did not know what the pretty dress meant that night would have dreamed it was but the mesh of a net made of white and gold.

But with all their pleasant manners it was evident the two girls looked upon us with a distinct aloofness. They glanced at us much as a brilliant bird of the air might be supposed to regard poultry, fowls of the cooped-up yard. Then they melted into the shadow of an archway behind the moonlit space, and we went on to another street and came upon little Sellamal, the harebell child; and, sitting down on the verandah which opens off the street, we heard her lessons as we have told, and got into conversation with her adopted mother.

We found her interested in listening to what we had to say about dedicating children to the service of the gods. She was extremely intelligent, and spoke Tamil such as one reads in books set for examination. It was easy to talk with her, for she saw the point of everything at once, and did not need to have truth broken up small and crumbled down and illustrated in half a dozen different ways before it could be understood. But the half-amused smile on the clever face told us how she regarded all we were saying. What was life and death earnestness to us was a game of words to her; a play the more to be enjoyed because, drawn by the sight of two Missie Ammals sitting together on the verandah, quite a little crowd had gathered and were listening appreciatively.

"That is your way of looking at it; now listen to my way. Each land in all the world has its own customs and religion. Each has that which is best for it. Change, and you invite confusion and much unpleasantness. Also by changing you express your ignorance and pride. Why should the child presume to greater wisdom than its father? And now listen to me! I will show you the matter from our side!" ("Yes, venerable mother, continue!" interposed the crowd encouragingly.) "You seem to feel it a sad thing that little Sellamal should be trained as we are training her. You seem to feel it wrong, and almost, perhaps, disgrace. But if you could see my eldest daughter the center of a thousand Brahmans and high-caste Hindus! If you could see every eye in that ring fixed upon her, upon her alone! If you could see the absorption – hardly do they dare to breathe lest they should miss a point of her beauty! Ah, you would know, could you see it all, upon whose side the glory lies and upon whose the shame! Compare that moment of exaltation with the groveling life of your Christians! Low-minded, flesh-devouring Christians, discerning not the difference between clean and unclean! Bah! And you would have my little Sellamal leave all this for that!"

"But afterward? What comes afterward?"

"What know I? What care I? That is a matter for the gods."

The child Sellamal listened to this, glancing from face to face with wistful, wondering eyes; and as I looked down upon her she looked up at me, and I looked deep into those eyes – such innocent eyes. Then something seemed to move the child, and she held up her face for a kiss.

This is only one temple town. There are many such in the South. These things are not easy to look at for long. We turn away with burning eyes, and only for the children's sake could we ever look again. . . .

A medical missionary, a woman of wide experience, was talking to a younger woman about the temple children. She had lived for some time, unknowingly, next door to a temple house in an Indian city. Night after night she said she was wakened by the cries of children – frightened cries, indignant cries, sometimes sharp cries as of pain. She inquired in the morning, but was always told the children had been punished for some naughtiness. "They were only being beaten." She was not satisfied, and tried to find out more through the police. But she feared the police were bribed to tell nothing, for she found out nothing through them. Later, by means of her medical work, she came full upon the truth.

THE THING WE FIGHT is not India or Indian, in essence or development. It is something alien to the old life of the people. It is not allowed in the Védas (ancient sacred books). It is like a parasite which has settled upon the bough of some noble forest tree – on it, but not of it. The parasite has gripped the bough with strong and interlacing roots; but it is not the bough.

We think of the real India as we see it in the thinker – the seeker after the unknown God, with his wistful eyes. "The Lord beholding him loved him," and we cannot help loving as we look. And there is the Indian woman hidden away from the noise of crowds, patient in her motherhood, loyal to the light she has. We see the spirit of the old land there; and it wins us and holds us, and makes it a joy to be here to live for India.

The true India is sensitive and very gentle. There is a wisdom in its ways, none the less wise because it is not the wisdom of the West. This spirit which traffics in children is callous and fierce as a ravening beast; and its wisdom descendeth not from above, but is earthly, sensual, devilish. . . . And this spirit, alien to the land, has settled upon it, and made itself at home in it, and so become a part of it that nothing but the touch of God will ever get it out. We want that touch of God: "Touch the mountains, and they shall smoke." That is why we write.

For we write for those who believe in prayer – not in the emasculated modern sense, but in the old Hebrew sense, deep as the other is shallow. We believe there is some connection between knowing and caring and praying, and what happens afterward. Otherwise we should leave the darkness to cover the things that belong to the dark. We should be forever dumb about them, if it were not that we know an evil covered up is not an evil conquered. So we do the thing from which we shrink with strong recoil; we stand on the edge of the pit, and look down and tell what we have seen, urged by the longing within us.

WE HAVE KNOWN of some little ones who, influenced by outside teaching, tried to escape the life they began to feel was wrong, but in each case they were overborne, for on the side of the oppressors there was power. I was in a temple house lately and noticed the doors – the massive iron-bossed doors are a feature of all well-built Hindu houses of the South. How could a little child shut up in such a room with its door shut, if need be, to the outside inquisitive world – how could she resist the strength that would force the garland round her neck? She might tear it off if she dared, but the little golden symbol had been hidden under the flowers, and the priest had blessed it; the deed was done – she was married to the god. And only those who have seen the effect of a few weeks of such a life upon a child, who has struggled in vain against it, can understand how cowed she may become, how completely every particle of courage and independence of spirit may be caused to disappear; and how what we had known as a bright, sparkling child, full of the fearless, confiding ways of a child, may become distrustful and constrained, quite incapable of taking a stand on her own account or of responding to any effort we might be able to make from outside. It is as if the child's spirit were broken, and those who know what she has gone through cannot wonder if it is.

"YOU ARE FIGHTING SATAN at a point upon which he is very sensitive; he will not leave you long in peace," wrote an experienced friend. On Palm Sunday, 1907, our first little band of young girls, fruit of this special work, confessed Christ in baptism, and we stood by the shining reach of water, and tasted of a joy so pure and thrilling that nothing of earth may be likened to it. A fortnight later we were ordered to the hills, and then the trouble came.

ANOTHER YEAR LIES BETWEEN the last chapter and this. For we can only write in odd corners of time, and sometimes time does not seem to have any odd corners. Quiet is even rarer. Just now I am sharing a room with seven very young people – the middle-aged babies we call them – and the only possible quiet is when they all elect to go to sleep together, a happiness not granted every day. The year that has passed since Indraneela left us has held some rainy days. But perhaps the little seed of the temple children's work must be watered much before it will spring and grow.

Perhaps, if we only knew it, all sheaves have such rain at the root. But today, as I look up from the writing to the dear little seven so kindly all asleep, and then through the western window with its glorious mountain view to the other nursery where the older little ones are settling down to their midday rice and curry, and when I stop to remember just where each might have been today if things had been otherwise, then I feel no watering could be too costly, if only in the end there may be the joy of sheaves.

The joy of sheaves – we have had it already; and when the time comes to tell the South Indian temple children's story in full, if God will, we will share it with you. The story is a story by itself. Before it can be told there must be much laborious digging in places out of sight. So we do not attempt more now than these few simple nursery chapters, written for the comfort of those, known and unknown, who are praying that something may be done. And there is larger comfort to offer: India is so great a word that in writing we confine ourselves on purpose to the South, but we rejoice to remember that elsewhere there are those whose eyes are open to look for these little children, and to work for them and save them. Soon we trust our dream will be fulfilled, and each province where the need is found to exist will have its own nursery, and its own band of volunteer Indian searchers.

For, in the South at least, the actual work of discovering the children must be done by the Indian workers. Most emphatically, no one else can do it.

LET US MAKE UP OUR MINDS to it and have done with wishing that things were easier. They are not, and they will not be. (So long as we fight Satan, he will fight us; if he does not, it will be because we are not worth fighting.)

3

Prayer Hunger

IF PRAYER MATTERS, then it ought not to be counted continually second in our scheme of life. . . . All the time the devil is fighting our half-hour's prayer; he never tires of fighting it. Sometimes there is a dullness which is a cloud of hell, sometimes a fiery assault.

THE *GLORIOSA SUPERBA* is native to South India. During the autumn rains you find it shooting in the lane bordered thickly by huge cactus and aloe. Here and there you see it in the open field. In the field it will have a chance, you think; but in the lane, crowded down by cactus and aloe, great strong assertive things with most fierce thorn and spike, what can a poor lily do but give in and disappear? A few weeks afterward you see a patch of color on the field, you go and gather handfuls of lovely lilies, and you revel in the tangle of color, a little bewilderment of delight. But the lane, go to the lane. There you see something far more satisfying: not only entangled color, but all the grace of form, God's full thought grown to perfection. Eight feet up in the clear air, bright against the luminous blue, unfurling its fire-flowers like banners of triumph, there is the lily victorious. Each little delicate bud and leaf seems as if filled with a separate keen little joy: the joy of just being beautiful and free.

The *Gloriosa* will exist in the field, as it will exist in the English hothouse, because it must. But it is not happy there. There is no proper development. Give it life, not just existence. Give it something to conquer. Give it the thorn and the spike.

Sometimes it may seem to us that our prayer life would develop more easily under easier conditions. The open field with no obstacle near – there the lily will surely thrive. Look at the plant again. In itself it is very fragile, but each leaf tapers tendril-wise, and asks for something, however sharp, if only it may curl round it and climb.

RECENTLY – so recently that it would be unwise to go into detail – we were in trouble about a little girl of ten or eleven, who, though not a temple child, was exposed to imminent danger and sorely needed deliverance. I happened to be alone at Dohnavur at the time and did not know what to answer to the child's urgent message: "If I can escape to you" (this meant if she braved capture and its consequences and fled across the fields alone at night), "can you protect me from my people?" To say "Yes" might have had fatal results. To say "No" seemed too impossible. . . .

Her case was complicated, if I may express it so, by the fact that though she knew very little – she had only had a few weeks' teaching and could not read – she had believed all we told her most simply and literally, and witnessed to her own people, whose reply to her had been: "You will see who is stronger, your God or ours! Do you think your Lord Jesus can deliver you from our hand or prevent us from doing as we choose with you? We shall see!" And the case of an older girl who had been, as those who knew her best believed, drugged and then bent to her people's will, was quoted: "Did your Lord Jesus deliver her? Where is she today? And you think he will deliver you!"

"But he will not let you hurt me," the child had answered fearlessly, though her strength was weakened even then by thirty hours without food; and, remembering one of the Bible stories she had heard during those weeks, she added, "I am Daniel, and you are the lions" – and she told them how the angel was sent to shut the lions' mouths. But she knew so little after all, and the bravest can be overborne, and she was only a little girl; so our hearts ached for her as we sent her the message: "You must not try to come to us. We cannot protect you. But Jesus is with you. He will not fail you. He says, 'Fear thou not, for I am with thee.'" That night they shut her up with a demon-possessed woman, that the terror of it might shake her faith in Christ. Next day they hinted that worse would happen soon. Our fear was lest her faith should fail before deliverance came.

Three and a half months of such tension as we have rarely known passed over us. . . .

God in very truth interposed in such fashion that everyone saw it was his hand, for no other hand could have done it. . . . Until the time comes when it may be more fully told to the glory of our God, we have hid it in our hearts. . . .

All through those months there was prayer for that child in India and in England. The matter was so urgent that we made it widely known, and some at least of those who heard gave themselves up to prayer; not to the mere easy prayer which costs little and does less, but to that waiting upon God which does not rest till it knows it has obtained access, knows that it has the petition that it desires of him. This sort of prayer costs.

MORE AND MORE AS WE GO ON, and learn our utter inability to move a single pebble by ourselves, and the mighty power of God to upturn mountains with a touch, we realize how infinitely important it is to know how to pray. There is the restful prayer of committal to which the immediate answer is peace. We could not live without this sort of prayer; we should be crushed and overborne, and give up brokenhearted if it were not for that peace. But the Apostle speaks of another prayer that is wrestle, conflict, "agony." And if these little children are to be delivered and protected . . . then some of us must be strong to meet the powers that will combat every inch of the field with us, and some of us must learn deeper things than we know yet about the solemn secret of prevailing prayer.

THERE IS A BARREN LAND which we reach when we have given all we have to give and feel drained to the last drop, and are plodding on without life or freshness, and our hearts are crying out for the quickening touch that renews us inwardly. We cannot live without that touch, and yet somehow we seem too spent to seek it. But we can stretch forth our hands, "I stretch forth my hands unto thee: my soul thirsteth after thee, as a thirsty land" (Ps. 143:6).

OUR LOVING LORD is not just present, but nearer than thought can imagine, so near that a whisper can reach him. You know the story of the man who had a quick temper and had not time to go away and pray for help. His habit was to send up a little telegraph prayer, "Thy sweetness, Lord!" and sweetness came.

Do you need courage? "Thy courage, Lord!" Patience? "Thy patience, Lord!" Love? "Thy love, Lord!" A quiet mind? "Thy quietness, Lord!" Shall we all practice this swift and simple way of prayer more and more? If we do, our Very Present Help will not disappoint us. For thou, Lord, hast never failed them that seek thee (Ps. 9:10).

PRAYER IN THE NAME of his beloved Son cannot lose its way in the void. It must find the ear of God.

For prayer is not emotion, it is a traffic between earth and heaven, "a commerce of love." Our ships set sail for heavenly shores; they do not return empty; it is impossible that they should; but we are not told what tide will bring them back. We think in terms of time; God thinks in terms of eternity. We see the near end of the thread on which are strung our moments, minutes, hours, days, like pearls on a string; the other end is out of view, and yet the thread is one, indivisible. We call the near end *time*, and the far end *eternity*, as though somewhere the thread broke (at death perhaps). But it is not so. We are living in eternity now.

THE MORE WE PONDERED over all that is said about prayer in the only book in the world that can speak with authority about it, the more we found to make us ask to be filled with the knowledge of his will before offering petitions for a desired good. When we were in doubt about his will (as we often were and are) and had not liberty to ask for a clear sign, there was the prayer of prayers ready framed for us: Thy will be done, whatever that will may be (Matt. 26:39).

I HAVE NOTICED that God sometimes waits until as a fellowship we wait on him about something. When we do that, things happen. Sometimes at the meeting there is a drag. Is our Father trying to show us that if he is to work wonders for us we *must* be in earnest about it, we *must* stir ourselves to lay hold of him? There are words in the Bible that make one wonder whether we do really as a company go very far in prayer. I want to go much further.

I KNOW WE HAVE ALL, for some time back, felt the need of something more in our prayer life. I have, personally, and I know others have, and there are the many in our family who come to prayer meetings because it is the custom to do so, but who are not urged by a great desire. It is the lack of prayer-hunger that often makes a big united meeting difficult. The one thing we seem to need most is a revived prayer life in our own souls – then the wave will flow out to the others.

"NOTHING HAD COME this month," [Dohnavur's secretary in England] wrote once, for her heart is always burdened for the little ones in danger of something so much more than pain and death, "so I began to pray for a hundred pounds. It sounded a very large sum, but I prayed. And yesterday Miss R. called. She put a check for a hundred pounds in my hand. She had had it by her for some time, but she had no light about how to use it, and then during the week – just when I was praying – she knew what the Lord wanted her to do; so she brought it to me. We have a very gentle, loving Father."

"But why not wish for a thousand pounds? That would make everything so nice and easy," said [one of our children] on hearing of the need to pray, and remembering the wish of the year before. But niceness and easiness would soon reduce the fibers of faith to jelly and pulp. . . . Peace was the first answer to our prayer, and soon afterward supplies were once more granted.

WHEN I AM IN PAIN or too tired to find words, I look at a picture of the Matterhorn and the lake at its foot, and I let it pray for me for you. Let the strength of the mountains be theirs, the purity of the snows, the beauty of the blue water, the steadfastness of the rocks, the loveliness of the flowers on the banks and, above all, the joy of the little stream that flows forth to bless others.

THE GATES OF ACCESS into the Father's presence are open continually. There is no need to push – perhaps "trying to pray" is sometimes a sort of pushing. This was how it came to me – *If the gates are open there is nothing to do but go in.* It sounds too simple to tell, but it helped me very much.

OFTEN THE ANSWER TO OUR PRAYER comes as it were obliquely. We pray for one, and the prayed-for one goes on apparently unimpressed. But the prayer, if one may put it so, glances off the soul that has hardened itself, and falls like a shower on another, and that soul responds like a watered garden, and blossoms out in flower.

THERE ARE TWO PRAYERS, one of which we are constantly praying, sometimes in words, sometimes in thoughts, always in actions. One is, "Teach me to do the thing that pleaseth *thee*" (Ps. 143:10); the other is, "Lord, let me do the thing that pleaseth *me*." . . . Some use the first in the morning, and the second all through the day;

for such, the second is the habit of the soul. Some vary between the two, and that leads to an up-and-down life. Some are growing more and more into the first as an all-day prayer, and their lives are growing stronger and gladder, more equable, more dependable, and much more peaceful.

4

Your Chief Love and Friend

LISTEN TO HIM, my children. He speaks to you, he
teaches you in a thousand ways every day. Through
the love of those who love you and live to help you, he
touches you, and he speaks to you. In the sunrise and the
sunset, and in moonlight, through the loveliness of the
things that he has made, through the thousand joys that
he plans for every one of you, through the sorrows that
come, too – in all these things, through all these things,
he who loved you unto death is speaking to you. Listen;
do not be deaf and blind to him; as you keep quiet and
listen, you will know deep down in your heart that you
are loved. As the air is round about you, so is his love

round about you now. It is enough. Trust that love to guide your lives. It will never, never fail.

OUTSIDE MY ROOM in Dohnavur a sunbird has hung her nest from a spray of valaris. The spray is as light as a spray of honeysuckle and grows in much the same careless way. The nest is attached to the spray by a few threads of cobweb, but so delicately that the touch of a child would detach it; a cupful of water thrown at it would sweep it down. It is a mere nothing of a nest. But it took a week of patient mothercraft to make it. It is roofed, it has a porch, and set deep within is a bed of silky down.

We know now that we were foolish, but we could not help being anxious about the fate of that wee home; for our northeast monsoon was due, and the nest hung in the eye of the wind and beyond the eaves of the house. There was no shelter from the wind and the rain. And how would the tiny mother find her food in the weather that would soon be upon us? The father bird would feed her if he could, but in rain the convolvulus and other nectar-carrying flowers are dashed and sodden. How could those little jewels on wings survive, much less bring up a family? It seemed as if bird wisdom for once were at fault.

The day the mother began to sit upon the two or three comfits that are her eggs, the monsoon broke. First came the wind; the spray swung from the branch and the nest swung from the spray. The wind did it no harm. Then the rain poured down in sheets; and still it swung in peace, for the four narrow leaves from whose axil the nest depended were so disposed that they turned into green gutters and carried off the water as quickly as it fell. Exactly where no rain could hurt it, that nest hung; and the little mother sat calmly through those floods, her dainty head resting on the threshold of the porch which she had made on the south side – the sheltered side. If a drop of water fell on her long, curved beak, she sucked it up as though it had been honey. And always, somehow, she was fed.

I think to more than one of us the Father spoke then. There is something very precious about a little bird and her nest, but "Ye are of more value than many sparrows" – than many sunbirds.

I WANT TO LEARN TO POUR OUT each several cupful of natural longing as well as natural love before the Lord. Almost every day gives a chance to do that.

IF MONOTONY TRIES ME, and I cannot stand drudgery; if stupid people fret me and little ruffles set me on edge; if I make much of the trifles of life, then I know nothing of Calvary love.

IF I AM INCONSIDERATE about the comfort of others, or their feelings, or even of their little weaknesses; if I am careless about their little hurts and miss opportunities to smooth their way; if I make the sweet running of household wheels more difficult to accomplish, then I know nothing of Calvary love.

IF INTERRUPTIONS ANNOY ME and private cares make me impatient; if I shadow the souls about me because I myself am shadowed, then I know nothing of Calvary love.

IF SOULS CAN SUFFER ALONGSIDE, and I hardly know it, because the spirit of discernment is not in me, then I know nothing of Calvary love.

IT IS A VERY GOOD THING to learn to take things by the right handle. An inward grouse is a devastating thing.

I expect you know this – we all do – but it is extraordinary how the devil tries to "get" us on the ordinary road of life. But all is well if only we are in God, deep in him, and he in us our daily strength and joy and song.

WE HAVE ALL KNOWN the gentle solace of human love. There has been a trouble, and we have braced ourselves to live through the day without letting anyone know. And then there was just a touch of a hand, or a word, or a penciled note – such a trifle; but that trifling thing was so unexpected, so undeserved, so brimful of what our beautiful old English calls tender mercies, that the heart melted before it, all the hurt gone. And there was a sense of something more. "Lord Jesus, what was it?" "My child, it was I; it is I."

I THINK OFTEN WE MISS MUCH by not being simple enough. Don't you think so? The little-child confidence is what God wants. It is true we are nothing, just nothing, but then he doesn't love us because we are something. He has called you. Of that I have not one atom of doubt, and whom he calls he justifies. . . . And go on, it is simply wonderful. "What shall we say then to these things? If

God be for us, who can be against us?" (Rom. 8:30–31).
Not even our own selves, our I that we feel is so distress-
ingly against all we long to be. Live in Romans 8 and let
the rest go by. That is your abiding place, not Romans 7.

"BUT WHEN HE WAS YET a great way off, his Father
saw him and had compassion, and ran, and fell on his
neck and kissed him" (Luke 15:20). So does our Father
see and run (O word of mystery!) to meet our heart's
deep longing; so does his love embrace. For he meets us
everywhere. If I am in trouble because of my sin, there
is forgiveness with thee, O my Father; if I am cast down,
with thee is lifting up; if I am athirst, with thee is eternal
refreshment. Always thy word to me is that tender word,
"Son, thou art ever with me, and all that I have is thine"
(Luke 15:31).

WE ALL KNOW that a curious sort of dullness can
creep over the soul at times, and I have been finding all
sorts of help in Psalm 30:11, which seems to have been
written for such occasions, and probably was. "Thou
hast turned my heaviness into joy; thou hast *torn off* my
sackcloth and girded me with gladness." Could anything

possibly be more delightful and more vigorous? I do like the "torn off."

So if any of us feel that scratchy sense of sackcloth on the inner man that makes for heaviness, let us change the tense, as we always may, and fastening our eyes on the Lord our Strength say, Lord, tear off my sackcloth, gird me with gladness, to the end that I – yea, even I – "may sing praise to thee, and not be silent."

GOD LOVES the "things that are not." We cannot be less than that. We cannot be less than an empty cockle shell lying on the beach. But the sea can flow over that shell and fill it full.

NOT IN ONE SUDDEN OUTPOURING, but rather with the quietness of light that falls upon our western hills and waters at eventide, a loveliness that she had often watched, Kohila came to the place where Christ and his love became her blessed all. She was still a shy soul. Deliverance from the kind of reserve which holds one back as by a silken thread was not hers yet, but it was coming. And those who loved her saw her opening, not as our blue morning glories and our white moonflowers open, as though moved by one gentle, all-pervading impulse, but more as our large purple passionflowers open, a little at a time. Their sepals and petals move separately and slowly, and there is a kind of stickiness about their stamens; they do not at once shake themselves free. But in the end, as you watch, you see them, and every other part of that symbolic flower, each in its several place. And the whole flower opens its heart to you and pours out its perfume.

CAST NOT AWAY therefore your confidence, which hath great recompense of reward. Cast it not away when grief is a companion with whom you must learn to become acquainted – "acquainted with grief"; the words are real now.

Two friends are bound together in love; the call to go to a foreign land for Christ comes to one; it does not come to the other. There must be renunciation then, or eternal loss. Or something even more poignant happens. Both hear the call; one goes abroad. The other prepares to follow. But the providence of God holds that one at home. Constraint that nothing can weaken holds the other abroad. Who can measure spiritual pain? Who can weigh the exceeding and eternal weight of glory that is being wrought while the eyes of faith are fixed, not on the pain, but on that which lies beyond it? But of this good thing they see nothing yet, not even the shadow. Only they know they will not serve their Lord together now.

Very tender comforts are prepared for such as these. They will find them as they go on.

FEELINGS CAN BE SHAKEN and the fight can be fearfully discouraging, for sometimes we seem to be losing ground and all seems to be going wrong. Then the devil comes and paints glorious pictures of what might have been. He did to me – I can see those pictures still. But as we go on steadfastly obeying the word that compelled, we do become aware that it is all worthwhile. We *know* it, we *know* Him with us, and that is life.

BUT IF WE ARE DEFEATED? "There is forgiveness with thee, that thou mayest be feared" (Ps. 130:4). When I was small I used to wonder why the word "feared" was used there; why not "loved"? But the Spirit of God chooses the words he uses in the scriptures, and there is a solemn truth in this word "feared." . . . It means the kind of love which has fear and reverence in it, and that kind of love will never think it is a little thing to grieve our holy God.

"AND HE HAD IN HIS RIGHT HAND seven stars. . . . And he laid his right hand upon me saying, 'Fear not'" (Rev. 1:16–17). Do you not sometimes find yourself almost thinking, "How can he, who has the whole world to care for, attend to this tiny matter that troubles me?" It seems almost unreasonable to ask for such attention. Sometimes it seems almost selfish. But here we have the truth we know so well in a great picture – the hand that holds the seven stars is the hand that is laid upon us.

YOU OFTEN REMIND ME of myself. Too much of your nature is exposed to the winds that blow upon it. You and I both need to withdraw more and more into the secret place with God. Do you know what I mean, I wonder?

OFTEN OUR FLASH OF HASTE means little. To read a book in an hour (if the book has taken half a lifetime to write) means nothing at all. To pray in a hurry of spirit means nothing. To live in a hurry means to do much but effect little. We build more quickly in wood, hay, and stubble than in gold, silver, and precious stones; but the one abides, the other does not.

If he who feels the world is too much with him will make for himself a little space, and let his mind settle like a bee in a flower on some great word of his God, and brood over it, pondering it till it has time to work in him, he will find himself in the greenwood.

THERE COMES A TIME when the personal falls from us and we cease from the weariness of being entangled and encumbered in ourselves and do, with all our hearts, desire to be perpetually lifted up in spirit above ourselves. But the trouble of a loved one can throw us into a fever of agitation. And yet to lose our peace is to lose our power to help. The energies which might have been turned to power are wasted in effectless grieving. Our very thoughts by their teasing reiteration, like low, eager voices that will not stop talking, tire us out. . . .

But there is a peace that must be ours if we are to prevail. "Peace I leave with you, my peace I give unto you: not as the world giveth, give I unto you. Let not your heart be troubled, neither let it be afraid" (John 14:27).

WE HAVE EACH OUR OWN private magic casement. The first glimpse of a snow mountain, or a stretch of purple heather, the tang of that same heather, the bittersweet scent of certain aromatic herbs, the sharp smell of seaweed, the soft breath of a meadow in clover, the sound of running waters, birds flying high in transparent blue, the first violet or primrose or patch of wood sorrel, a cushion of ferny moss, a spray of wild rose – the heart knoweth its own casement. For some of us in Dohnavur it is just the whistle of the Malabar thrush.

This bird is a friend of rocks and rivers in deep woods, and when we go to our forest on the mountains, we know that the blissful moment between sleeping and waking of our first morning in that beloved place will thrill to the clear whistle just outside our windows, and we shall be caught away on the wings of a dream – whither? Who can tell? Only we know the casement is open and the air is golden and full of the flutings of a bird.

But it may be far from golden in the forest. It may be wild weather. Then slashing rain whips the low, tiled roof, and furious gusts tearing down the ravine threaten to uproot the houses that have dared to perch up there. The branches of the trees strike each other with a sound of loud complaining. Their leaves are colorless. A palm, thrusting through his lesser neighbors, tosses black plumes like ostrich feathers against the gray smear that is the sky. On such a morning a heavy gloom broods over the forest, a gloom like a pall. The place may be swept with cloud, or smothered in mist, and there may not be one cheerful thing to look at anywhere, except the log fire on the open hearth, and probably it smokes.

It may be a most melancholy morning, but nothing makes any difference to that bird. He whistles his inconsequent tune, never twice the same, never hurried; it is the most leisurely thing imaginable. The key is continually changing (like life). You cannot follow him or ever anticipate him; you can only listen and love him.

ON A RAINY DAY IN THE FOREST after the first burst of the monsoon is over, a surprising thing is often seen. The rain then is . . . quite heavy enough, one would think, to destroy in a moment such a fragile thing as a butterfly.

And yet you may see the black-and-yellow *Papilio minos* of the forest out in the wet, hovering over the flowery bushes, lighting on one for a dripping moment, then fluttering off and across some open space. The spread of her wings is five or six inches from tip to tip;

you watch half incredulously those five or six inches
of delicate tissue borne down perhaps, sometimes, but
always rising again, soaring again.

If God can make his birds to whistle in drenched and
stormy darkness, if he can make his butterflies able to
bear up under rain, what can he not do for the heart that
trusts him?

WE RETURNED FROM THAT VILLAGE knowing
that we had been walking over roads where our Lord had
walked before we had even heard of the place. What if
suddenly, on the soft carpets in great houses, on the well-
swept city streets, on the highways and the byways of
smaller towns and scattered little villages, on the decks
of great ships, on the very waters about them and in
the room where we work today, these unseen footprints
should appear, how would it be? But our seeing them
would make them no more there than they are now.

WITHOUT HIM, LOVER OF ALL LOVERS, life is dust.
With him it is like the rivers that run among the hills,
fulfilled with perpetual surprises.

5

Forget Yourself in Serving Others

GOD GIVES LOVE; it isn't in us to love. I don't naturally
love people I don't know (and I don't naturally love all
the people I do know!). Love is of God and from God,
and he pours it into our hearts if we let him.

STAND BY YOUR FELLOWSHIP and family, and forget
yourself in serving others. That is the way of joy.

SOME OF YOU WHO ARE LONGING to live this life
still hesitate. There is no life in all the world so joyful. It
has pain in it, too, but looking back I can tell you truly,

there is far more joy than pain. Do not hesitate. Give yourselves wholly to your Lord to be prepared for whatever he has chosen for you to do.

BEFORE THE CHILDREN CAME, we were continually camping in tents, mud huts, or tumbledown old bungalows, and we never stopped to grow even a flower; but after they came, we had to make a home for them, so things were different. And because we know that beautiful things are dear to God (look deep into beauty and you see him there), and that ugly, vulgar, coarse things are a jar, like a false note in music, we chose, when we had the choice, the beautiful, not the ugly. Someone (the angels perhaps) had planted trees up and down the field for us. We cherished those trees. And flowers began to grow where only scrub had been, and gradually the place became sweet and green, almost as though it offered coolness. And the bare, red blot on the bare, hot plain changed to something pleasant to the eye and beloved, at least to ourselves.

THE ROOMS ARE INDIAN, unfurnished save for cupboards, brass vessels and, according to the nice upper-class habit of the South, grass mats for beds; and the red-tiled floors are kept shiny by constant washing. Later on we found shells on the beach at Cape Comorin and water-worn wood like carved work by the river in the forest; and the children learned to dress their rooms with this inexpensive loveliness.

WHEN WE WERE AN ITINERATING BAND, we had many offers from Christian girls and women to join us, as many in one month as we now have in five years. Sometimes it has seemed to us that we were set to learn and to teach a new and difficult lesson, the sacredness of the commonplace. Day by day we learn to rub out a little more of the clear chalked line that someone has ruled on life's blackboard; the secular and the spiritual may not be divided now. The enlightening of a dark soul or the lighting of a kitchen fire, it matters not which it is, if only we are obedient to the heavenly vision, and work with a pure intention to the glory of our God.

WE HAVE FOUND IT POSSIBLE to be directed as a company so that we can move together in a harmony of spirit that is restful and very sure. A company has to wait longer than one or two might have to do, but if all be set on doing their Lord's will and be truly one in loyalty and the New Testament kind of affection that makes each one feel safe with each other one, if all flow together to the goodness of the Lord, unanimity is certain. . . . And we have always found that before the ultimate word must be spoken, divergent thoughts have vanished, as by some peaceful magic. The interval is sure to be perplexed by a temptation to the futile fuss of talk. Recognize this for what it is, the influence of the adversary (for hurry of spirit confuses), and before long the same quiet word will come to all.

THE ACCALS, without whom this work in all its various branches could not be undertaken, are a band of Indian sisters (the word *accal* means older sister) who live for the service of the children. First among the Accals is Ponnammal (Golden). With the quick affection of the East the children find another word for gold and call her doubly Golden Sister. . . .

Ponnammal's work lies chiefly among the convert-nurses and the babies. She has charge of the nurseries and of the food arrangements, so intricate and difficult to the mere lay mind; she trains her workers to thoroughness and earnestness, and by force of example seems to create an atmosphere of cheerful unselfishness that is very inspiring. How often we have sent a young convert, tempted to self-centeredness and depression, to Ponnammal, and seen her return to her ordinary work braced and bright and sensible. We are all faulty and weak at times, and every nursery, like every life, has its occasional lapses; but on the whole it is not too much to say that the nurseries are happy places, and Ponnammal's influence goes through them all like a fresh wind. And this in spite of very poor health. For Ponnammal, who was the leader of our itinerating band, broke down hopelessly, and thought her use in life had passed – till the babies came and brought her back to activity again. And the joy of the Lord, we have often proved, is strength for body as well as soul. . . .

Ponnammal lost all her little fortune by joining us. She could, perhaps, have recovered it by going to law, but she did not feel it right to do so, and she suffered herself to be defrauded. "How could I teach others to be unworldly if I myself did what to them would appear worldly-minded?" That was all she ever said by way of explanation.

SELLAMUTTU, WHO COMES NEXT to Ponnammal, is the "Pearl" of previous records, and she has been a pearl to us through all our years together. She is special Accal to the household of children above the baby-age – a healthy, high-spirited crowd of most diverse dispositions; and she is loved by one and all with a love which is tempered with great respect, for she is "all pure justice," as a little girl remarked feelingly not long ago, after being rather sharply reproved for exceeding naughtiness: "within my heart wrath burned like a fire; but my mouth could not open to reply, for inside me a voice said, 'It is true, entirely true; Accal is perfectly just.'"

NO MONEY WOULD HAVE DRAWN these workers to us. Work which has no clear ending, but drifts on into the night if babies are young or troublesome – such work makes demands upon devotion and practical unselfishness which appeal to none but those who are prepared to love with the tireless love of the mother. . . .

Yet we find that the work, though so demanding, is full of compensations. The convert in her loneliness is welcomed into a family where little children need her and will soon love her dearly. The uncomforted places in her heart become healed, for the touch of a little child is very healing. If she is willing to forget herself and live for that little child, something new springs up within her; she does not understand it, but those who watch her know that all is well. Sometimes long afterward she reads her own heart's story and opens it to us. "I was torn with longing for my home. I dreamed night after night about it, and I used to waken just wild to run back. And yet I knew if I had, it would have been destruction to my soul. And then the baby came, and you put her into my arms, and she grew into my heart, and she took away all that feeling, till I forgot I ever had it." This was the story of one, a young wife, for whom the natural joys of home can never be.

But if there is selfishness or slackness or a weak desire to drift along in easiness, taking all and giving nothing, things are otherwise. For such the nurseries hold nothing but noise and interruptions. We ask to be spared from such as these. Or if they come, may they be inspired by the constraining love of Christ and "The Glory of the Usual."

TO BELONG to the Sisters of the Common Life will certainly bring the devil's fire upon us. . . . When a soul sets out to find God, it does not know whither it will come, and by what path it will be led; but those who catch the vision are ready to follow the Lamb whithersoever he goeth. . . . As Sisters of the Common Life we are trusted to be very careful about our inner discipline, and continually to expose every part of our inward life to the searching light of God. . . .

We are trusted *to spread the spirit of love.* Tenderness in judgment, the habit of thinking the best of one another, unwillingness to believe evil, grief if we are forced to do so, eagerness to believe good, joy over one recovered from any slip or fall, unselfish gladness in another's joys, sorrow in another's sorrow, readiness to do anything to help another entirely irrespective of self – all this and much more is included in that wonderful word *love.*

If love weakens among us, if it ever becomes possible to tolerate the least shadow of an unloving thought, our fellowship will begin to perish. Unlove is deadly. It is a cancer. It may kill slowly but it always kills in the end. Let us fear it, fear to give room to it as we should fear to nurse a cobra. It is deadlier than any cobra. And just as one minute drop of the almost invisible cobra venom spreads swiftly all over the body of one into whom it has been injected, so one drop of the gall of unlove in my heart or yours, however unseen, has a terrible power of spreading all through our family, for we are one body – we are parts of one another. If one member suffers loss, all suffer loss. Not one of us liveth to herself.

We owe it to the younger ones to teach them the truth that united prayer is impossible unless there be loyal love. If unlove be discovered anywhere, stop everything and put it right, if possible at once.

O MY CHILDREN, if only you would make up your minds never to doubt the love of another sister or brother in Christ, but *always* to think the best and never admit an unkind thought in your heart, how happy, how heavenly, life would be.

I REMEMBER ONCE weeks of unhappiness because a certain curry was badly cooked – the cause could have been discovered in five minutes if only there had been loving frankness, and speaking *to* instead of speaking *of* the one who made that curry.

I CANNOT REST because of the distress that comes to me as I think of a misunderstanding that need never have been between two of you who love the Lord Jesus and are wholly given to his service. . . .

Often these misunderstandings are about the merest trifles. You let them grow and grow till your whole day is shadowed. This delights the devil, but it terribly injures your own soul, and it sorely grieves the spirit of love. Also, and this is serious, while you are yielding to such feelings you are unconsciously sowing seeds of unlove and distrust in other hearts – in the children's hearts. These seeds will spring to life and grow up to your sorrow one day.

Why don't you keep the Law of the Family and go straight to the one who has (you think) done something wrong? You can't, do you say? You can. Love will find a way.

SO WE ALWAYS CAME TO THIS: Go on loving: "By the words of thy lips have I guarded me from hard ways" (the Septuagint rendering of Ps. 77:4). Go on praying: Pray for them that despitefully use you. (Our Lord does not say, "Wait till they are sorry for treating you so.") . . .

Be careful also of your after-thinking as well as of your after-talking about any who have misjudged you. "The hill-man thinks upon the beauty of his hills; the farmer thinks upon his fields that have yielded him rich crops; the good think on the boons bestowed by worthy men; the base man's thoughts are fixed on the abuse he has received," is another old Tamil saying. Do not feed unloving thoughts. Remember His word, "I forgave thee all that debt."

THIS "I" THAT IS MYSELF can disturb our very holiest things. The passionate longing (for it is indeed a passion and a pain) to be the one to rise and serve is the last thing to die in the heart that loves its fellows and finds its joy in serving them, just as the last prayer we drop is the prayer that we (with an emphasis on the *we*) may be used.

Is this a hard saying? But why? The pen on the desk is kept clean and filled with ink. The pencil is kept pointed. Both are ready, both are at hand; sometimes one is used, sometimes the other; if only the work be done, what does it matter which does it? There can be a subtle selfishness, a kind of covetousness which is idolatry (of self) in the perpetual cry, "Use *me*."

HAVE YOU EVER THOUGHT how infectious fear can be? It spreads from one to another more quickly and certainly than any of the fevers we know so well. So, for the sake of others, let us refuse the spirit of fear which God never gives us (if he does not, who does?), and let us open our hearts wide to the spirit "of power and love and discipline" (2 Tim. 1:7). We can do this if we will.

Thank God, courage is as infectious as discouragement. Have you not often felt the cheer and strength that seem to flow from one whose mind is stayed on God? I have.

And I have been thinking of another, a greater, reason for refusing the spirit of fear. When we are downhearted, or fearful, or weak, we are saying to everybody, by looks and by deeds if not by words, "After all, our Lord is not to be absolutely trusted." Somewhere near us, though we do not see them, are others, the good angels and the spirits of evil. To them, too, when we yield to fear, we say the same dishonoring thing. So for the greater glory of our glorious Savior who has never once failed us, and never will fail us, who has loved and led and guarded us all these years, let us look to him now and pray from the ground of our heart, "Lord, give us valor."

WHEN YOU ARE FEELING DOWNHEARTED, go and do something for others. If you do that, and go on doing it, you will come to the place where Habakkuk was when he wrote his glorious *Yet*. "Although the fig tree shall not blossom, neither shall fruit be in the vines; the labor of the olive shall fail, and the fields shall yield no meat; the flock shall be cut off from the fold, and there shall be no herd in the stalls: *Yet* I will rejoice in the Lord; I will joy in the God of my salvation" (Hab. 3:17–18).

Think of the grit of that man long ago. He did not wail about feelings. And his God is your God. He can make even you a Habakkuk.

I WONDER IF YOU FEEL AS I DO about the heavenliness of song. I believe truly that Satan cannot endure it, and so slips out of the room – more or less! – when there is true song.

THE REASON WHY SINGING is such a splendid shield against the fiery darts of the devil is that it greatly helps us to forget him, and he cannot endure being forgotten. He likes us to be occupied with him, with what he is doing (our temptations), with his victories (our falls), with anything but our glorious Lord. So sing. Never be afraid of singing too much.

IT MATTERS A GOOD DEAL that your book-food should be strong meat. We are what we think about. Think about trivial things or weak things and somehow one loses fiber and becomes flabby in spirit.

CAN WE EVER THANK GOD ENOUGH for the spirit of happiness? . . . There is something in the continuance of happiness in untoward circumstances that is like the power of rejuvenescence in the rotifer. This little creature, which we find sometimes by scores in a drop of water, is a thing so delicate that a slip of the cover-glass on the slide will destroy the pinpoint of life in its crystal vase. And yet, when the pond dries up, it can gather itself into a ball within which are the forces of life. Then after being blown about by the wind perhaps for years, in a state of utter dustiness, when the rotifer finds itself in its own element the ball will revive, and put forth foot and head and silver wheel, and be as it was before, a minute marvel of activity and apparent enjoyment. The spirit of happiness is sheer miracle.

WHAT A JOYFUL LIFE OURS IS, continually proving God's tenderness in the very little things. There is nothing too small for him to help.

SIMPLE, EFFORTLESS INTIMACY, that closeness of touch which is friendship indeed, is surely possible. But rather we would put it otherwise, and say that without it service together, of the only sort we would care to know, is perfectly impossible.

In our work all along we have had this joy to the full. God in his goodness gave us from the first those who responded at once to the confidence we offered them. In India the ideal of a consecrated life is a life with no reserves – which seeks for nothing, understands nothing, cares for nothing but to be poured forth upon the sacrifice and service. . . .The spring of heart to heart that we call affinity, the knitting no hand can ever afterward unravel – these experiences have been granted to us all through our work together, and we thank God for it.

I HAVE BEEN THINKING THIS – don't get too heavy in talk and prayer. Earnestness does not necessarily mean heaviness. It is the *joy* of the Lord that is strength.

I PRAY FOR YOU ALL, for each one of you as if there were no other. Never feel lost in a crowd. It is not so. Each one of you is precious.

6

Poetry of Childhood

TWO FABLES OFTEN CAME TO MIND in those first days. When we were perplexed by diverse advisers (for we found that both books and people differed considerably about the proper way to bring up children), then we thought of Aesop's old man and his donkey. And when we hardly dared to do anything for fear of doing wrong, the mother-bear story . . . was delightfully in point: "Shall I," said the bear's cub to his mother, "move my right paw first or my left, or my two front paws together, or the two hind ones, or all four at once, or how?"

"Leave off thinking, and walk," grunted the old bear.

So in a great simplicity we tried to let the children

grow as the green things about them grew, not too closely regarded, not pulled up at frequent intervals to see how they were getting on.

A TEACHER WAS OFFERED TO US who appeared to be all that we wanted, and the hardest thing we had to do that year was to return her to the one who had so kindly sent her to us. Another came, but we could not use her either, and we had to close the kindergarten. . . . It was as though something in the place acted as touchstone and declared what was, as apart from what seemed to be, in these whom we would so gladly have used because we needed them so much. In each case truth was the rock upon which they foundered. If our children were to grow up truthful they must be taught by those who had a regard for truth; and not just a casual regard, a *delicate* regard. On this point we were adamant.

AFTER A WHILE INDOORS we used to go out into the garden. It was Wonderland to the children. We never suggested questions and never answered any that they did not ask (we had as much as we could do to find answers to those they did ask) but we, as it were, ran to meet their minds in welcome. It was a merry kind of schooling.

AS THEY GREW OLDER, we tried, by means of travelling on the King's business, and with the splendid help of books, to enlarge our children's minds so that they would be always eager to learn more. And we learned more than we taught.

WE HEARD OF HER FIRST through our good Pakium, who, during a pilgrimage round the district, paid a visit to the family of which she was the youngest member. "She lay in her cradle asleep" – Pakium kindled over it – "like an innocent little flower, and she once opened her eyes – such eyes! – and smiled up in my face. Oh, like a flower is the babe!" And much speech followed, till we pictured a tender, flower-like baby, all sweetness and smiles.

Her story was such as to suggest fears, though on the surface things looked safe. Her grandfather, a fine old man, head of the house, was sheltering the baby and her mother and three other children; for the son-in-law had "gone to Colombo," which in this case meant he desired to be free from the responsibilities of wife and family. He had left no address, and had not written after his departure. So the old man had the five on his hands. A temple woman belonging to a famous South-country temple,

knowing the circumstances, had made a flattering offer
for the baby, then just three months old. The grandfather
had refused; but the grandmother was religious, and she
felt the pinch of the extra five, and secretly influenced
her daughter, so that it was probable the temple woman
would win if she waited long enough. And temple women
know how to wait.

A year passed quietly. We had friends on the watch,
and they kept us informed of what was going on. The
idea of dedication was becoming gradually familiar to
the grandfather, and he was ill and times were hard. But
still we could do nothing, for to himself and his whole
clan adoption by Christians was a far more unpleasant
alternative than temple dedication. After all, the temple
people never break caste. . . .

We were sitting round the dinner table one wet
evening, thinking of nothing more exciting than the
flying and creeping creatures which insisted upon drown-
ing themselves in our soup, when the jingle of bullock
bells made us look at each other incredulously; and then,
without waiting to wonder who it was, we all ran out
and met Rukma running in from the wet darkness. "It's
it! It's it!" she cried, and danced into the dining room,
decorum thrown to the pools in the compound. "Look at

it!" And we saw a bundle in her arms. And it howled.

From that day on for nearly a week it continued consistently to howl. . . . The very crows made remarks about the baby when she wakened the morning with her howls. Mercifully for the family's nerves she fell asleep at noon; but as soon as she woke she began again, and went on till both she and we were exhausted. There were no tears, the big dark eyes were only entirely defiant; and the baby stood straight up with her hands behind her back and her mouth open – that was all. But we knew it meant pure misery, though expressed so very aggressively; and we coaxed and petted when she would allow us, and won her confidence at last, and then she stopped.

It took months to tame the little thing. She had been allowed to do exactly as she liked; for she was her grandfather's pet, and no one might cross her will. We had to go very gently; but eventually she understood and became a dear little girl, reserved but very affectionate, and scampish to such a degree that Chellalu, discerning a congenial spirit, decided to adopt her as "her friend."

This fact was announced to us at the babies' Bible class, when the word "friend," which was new to the babies, was being explained. It has four syllables in Tamil, and the babies love four-syllabled words. They were rolling this juicy morsel under their tongues with sounds of appreciation, when Chellalu pointed across to Naveena, and with an air of possession remarked, "*She* is my friend." The other babies nodded their heads, "Yes, Naveena is Chellalu's friend!" Naveena looked flattered and very pleased.

These friends in a kindergarten class are rather terrible. They are always separated – as the Tamil would say, if one sits north the other sits south – but even so there are means of communication. This morning, passing the door of the kindergarten room, I looked in and saw something not included in the timetable. We have a little yellow bellflower here which grows in great profusion; and some vandal taught the babies to blow it up like a little balloon, and then snap it on the forehead. The crack it makes is delightful. We do not like this game, and try to teach the babies to respect the pretty flowers; but there are so many sins in the world, that we do not make another by actually forbidding it; we trust to time and sense and good feeling to help us. So it comes to pass that the worst scamps indulge in this game without feeling too guilty; and now I saw Chellalu with a handful of the flowers, cracking them at intervals, to the distraction of the teacher and the delight of all the class. One other was cracking flowers too. It was Naveena, and there was a method in her cracks. When Rukma turned to Chellalu, Naveena cracked her flower. When she turned to Naveena, then Chellalu cracked hers.

THERE WERE LITTLE ONES, TOO, and Indian sister-workers who required change and rest and refreshment as much as we did. What were we to do? We looked up to the Lord, our leader, and then we looked up to the hills that lay so near Dohnavur. . . .

Elephants haunted those uplands, and bears and tigers, sambur, wild pigs, deer, the ever-fascinating monkey, the huge monitor lizard like a toy crocodile, and countless furred and feathered marvels. Life was all gladness there. Once the children, entranced, saw a tigress at play with her cubs. They rushed down to call me, but the tigress heard their cries of joy and took her cubs elsewhere; and once one of us met a tiger full face, but he, too, politely moved away. Later, we were to meet panthers, wild dogs, bears, and other forest people – not every day, but often enough to lend zest to life. And the children, and we with them, scrambled up dizzy rocks to almost inaccessible places, to the amazement of the foresters, who had not seen before, they said, such adventurous children. This was nectar to me. And indeed they were splendid climbers and never knew fear. Cool air, climbs, heavenly views, a mountain river, ferns, flowers, mosses (cushiony moss was a special pleasure; it does not grow on the plains) – what was there left to wish?

A dear little story is connected in my mind with our first visit to that woodland place. We left Dohnavur one evening in the heat of early September, and spent a breathless night in a forest hut under the hills. Next morning, the children set off to walk the three thousand feet to the house, leaving me to follow. . . . The way was long, and it was evening when I reached a stream not far from the house and stopped to rest. . . . And then from the other side of the stream I heard merry laughter, and shouts of welcome, and the children flew across like a flock of blue forest birds, and there were kisses and embraces so eager and so loving that we might have been parted for weeks. Then in the evening light that filled the air with gold-shine, we all went up to the house, and my tiredness fell from me in the happiness of being with the children again. It was one of those earthly pictures of heavenly things that cannot be forgotten.

SICK BIRDS AND STRAYED BIRDS are our most usual pets. We have not the heart to shut up wild things in cages, except when they are invalided or too young to fend for themselves. When they are considered well enough or old enough to be set at liberty, there is general jubilation. But alas! The little sunbird that has licked honey for a fortnight from affectionate fingers is apt to acquire too trustful a disposition for life in a world infested by hard-pressed pariah dogs. "The babies are our longest lasting pets," one small mourner was heard confiding to another after the tragic deaths of several little favorites. "I am glad there is no wild beast that wants to eat them up."

Animals would be much to the fore if only we could suitably have them. "When I am grown up," said one, undaunted by accidents, "I shall have twenty dogs and twenty cats, and they shall play with each other." Ten minutes after she had made this announcement I found her chuckling to herself, as with a child's vivid imagination she surveyed the diverting prospect. . . .

Occasionally the dolls, who for the most part live in boxes, are produced and hung in cradles swung from the trees. The effect of a dozen or so of these little hammocks, made of bits over from their own little garments, is very comical. Houses are arranged for the sleepers, to be ready when they wake. These houses follow the bungalow type. There is a central room "for food and meetings," and two bedrooms, one on each side. There is a verandah, with steps, and a curl meant for decorative architecture finishes either side of the steps. The kitchen, Indian fashion, is at a little distance. As all this is made of mud, patted into shape, on the raised model plan, with very low walls and spaces for doors, you may easily make a mistake and overlook the walls when invited to pay a visit. Nothing more offends the general sense of propriety. "You have stepped over the wall. That is wall. The door is on the other side. Please come in by the door."

Grown-up people, though so stupid, have some redeeming features. It is they who give the dolls. Also they kindly mend them when, as often happens, limbs come off. Here, judging by previous experience, one would expect a great display of sympathy with the sorely injured treasure. There is nothing of the sort. Strong common sense comes to the rescue, and the most heroic operative measures are regarded with perfect equanimity. The maternal mind thus disengaged has time to moralize. "Are you mending my doll's leg to the glory of God?" was a question put to Mrs. Walker one day.

NEW LIGHT ON OLD TEXTS might be the safe and sober title to a chapterful of sundries. "Do you know about the devil's beginning?" This was Leela to the Firefly, whose eager "Tell me, Leela!" started Leela at a trot. . . .

"In the beginning," began Leela in unctuous tones, "the bad devil was good. He was an angel. He lived in heaven. One day all the angels came to sing to God. Then the devil was angry. He got angrier and angrier. He was very rude to God." Here Leela seemed to freeze all over, and her voice sounded quite deep and awful. Irreverence was far from her intention. "That bad, bad devil said: 'I won't stand before God's chair any more, and I won't sing to God any more. *I want to sit in God's chair, and make God sing to me!*'" There was a perfectly horrified pause, as the enormity of the transgression became evident. "So God took him, and tumbled him down out of heaven, and he was turned into the devil."

There was another solemn pause, then Leela continued cheerfully, "And we each have a little devil; he says, 'Tell lies, steal, be cross.' And we each have a little angel; he says, 'Don't tell lies, don't steal, don't be cross.' That devil is a nasty little devil."

"Which is more necessary," inquired the practical

Firefly of the Elf who just then appeared, "our little angel, or our Ammal?" (mother).

"Well," returned the Elf impartially, "I think both are necessary. Our little angel is very important; he looks at God's face for us. But then Jesus knows we couldn't do without a mother. So he gives us both." There was a vehement raid upon me, and the book which was considered too absorbing was triumphantly carried off.

"It was nice and kind of Jesus," said little Leela in cooing tones; "when I see him I will run up to him fast, and give him hugs and kisses."

"But he is God," said one of the small elders soberly.

"But he is our Lord Jesus too," said another quickly, feeling for Leela, whose loving little heart had meant nothing wrong. Leela looked grateful, and afterward confided that she always gave him kisses in her prayers.

Then from these heights there was a sudden drop. "I want to see the bad devil *a corpse,*" said the Firefly, with startling energy.

BUT THE TIME OF ALL TIMES to get into the very inside mind of an Indian child is in the wonderful sunset hour when all nature breathes softly, and just a little later, when the stars come out. Sometimes one gets shocks.

I had always thought children heard God's voice in the thunder and were awed. Not at all. "The clouds are quarrelling. If they don't take care they'll spill," was the painfully practical remark that blew the dust from my eyes. So even in the silent glory of sunset, and even under the solemn stars, one must be prepared for prose as well as poetry. . . .

Often now an excited little creature comes flying in, impetuous, full of some new discovery. Once it was a beetle rolling a ball much bigger than himself to a hiding place under a tree. The children wanted to help the beetle, and they made a smooth track for him; but he obstinately persisted in kicking it by the rough way of his choice. Once it was a weed, as we disrespectfully call our flower guests who come without being invited. "It has thirteen different colors, not counting the stalk." Once it was a praying mantis, whose devotional manners charmed the whole community and suggested any number of moral reflections. Often it is a new mimic insect, like a straw, or a leaf, or a bit of bark. Once it was green clouds.

"Green clouds! Oh, you little green girl!" I said not in the least believing. But the earnest, "*Indeed,* they are green," and the tugging little hands prevailed. The clouds were really green; a sort of undefined sea-green, like the color of a wave before it rolls over, just as the crest curls ready to break. They were lighted with lemon color toward the under edge, and darkened into gray above, and they were floating in violet air. Then through that pure violet the sickle of the new moon curved, sharp against its transparency. Jupiter, at some seasons very large and brilliant here, shone above the moon; and the little filmy cloudlets swept across it, making halos as they passed.

The splendor and the silence of the movement held us still. I think we both felt we might miss something if we spoke. Slowly the lemon light faded; the cloud colors melted into a blue that was almost electric. Every moment the moon cut clearer, and the silver of the planet grew more radiant. And the little halos flying round it were like rainbows caught and twisted into rings.

At last the child spoke, her brown eyes fixed wistfully on the fading glory of the sky. "I thought he was coming back," she said. Then I found she had fancied to herself that our Lord went home on a sunset cloud, pink and soft and beautiful, with gold from the inside shining through. "And whenever the clouds are just like that, I look to see if he is not there. And I have looked so often, and he hasn't come yet." But other little voices broke in upon us – "What is the sky made of? Is it a real roof? Look at the big star! Oh, it is *running!* Where is it running to? Why has it got a colored crown?"

In the warm southland the spirit of the moonlight and the starlight need not be shut out unkindly. We sit outside with it and sleep outside beside it. The toil and the littleness of the day pass out of memory in that large calm, as the heat that has passed is forgotten in the cool. The juniors generally go to bed early, but sometimes they break bounds and sit on the sand in the courtyard, in the starshine, very wide awake. Then, if you happen to be conveniently exhausted and unfit for conversation, the compassionate children will leave you in peace and forget your near existence. You have the chance then, if you care to take it, to drop for awhile into the world that is never far away, though we so seldom seem to find the little bypath into it.

"I want to string all the stars together on a thread and make a necklace." This was Lola.

"You can't," said the Firefly, scandalized. "They aren't yours."

"Whose are they?" Lola sounded defiant.

"They're God's. They're the lamps of God's village."

"Where is God's village?"

"Up there."

"What is it called?"

"It's Heaven, of course."

"And it's up there?"

Lola pointed up with one fat forefinger, and looked searchingly at the Firefly, who answered with confidence, "Yes, up there; high up."

Then Lola . . . gathered herself together and demanded, "How does it stay up?"

I WONDER WHAT your biggest temptation is. Is it to be suddenly angry? That was mine when I was a little girl. I used to feel something like a fire suddenly burning up in my heart. If you feel like that, ask the Lord Jesus to pour his cool, kind, gentle love into your heart instead. Never go on being angry with anyone; be Jesus' little peacemaker.

IN OUR MOUNTAIN RAVINE, just above our swimming pool, a small tree grows on the rock in midstream. When the river is in flood and a roaring torrent pours over the little tree, whipping off its every leaf, it stands unmoved. Its roots grip the rock. We wanted the children to be like that.

When sudden illness struck five-year-old Lulla, Amy sent for a doctor. He came immediately but arrived too late.

IT WAS IN THAT CHILLY HOUR between night and morning. A lantern burned dimly in the room where Lulla lay; there was nothing in that darkened room to account for what we saw. The child was in pain, struggling for breath, turning to us for what we could not give. I left her with Mabel Wade and Ponnammal, and, going to a side room, cried to our Father to take her quickly.

I was not more than a minute away, but when I returned she was radiant. Her little lovely face was lighted with amazement and happiness. She was looking up and clapping her hands as delighted children do. When she saw me she stretched out her arms and flung them round my neck, as though saying goodbye, in a hurry to be gone; then she turned to the others in the same eager way, and then again, holding out her arms to someone whom we could not see, she clapped her hands. . . .

We looked where she was looking, almost thinking that we should see what she saw. What must the fountain of joy be if the spray from the edge of the pool can be like that? When we turned the next bend of the road, and the sorrow that waited there met us, we were comforted, words cannot tell how tenderly, by this that we had seen when we followed the child almost to the border of the land of joy.

7

Embracing God's Will

IN THE EARLIER YEARS of the work in Dohnavur we were constantly reminded of how there came a messenger unto Job and said . . . And while he was yet speaking there came also another, and said . . . (Job 1:13–19) – for trouble followed trouble very much after the fashion of those messengers.

One evening, in a brief lull between the messengers, two of us spent an hour with a small telescope looking at the Great Nebula in Orion. As I looked into those deeps of darkness lighted by an infinitely far and faint pale flame, a sense of the eternal came upon me. "The world passeth away and the lust thereof" – and the grief thereof, and the wrong thereof – "but he that doeth the will of God abideth forever" (1 John 2:17), was the word of that breath of flame. The transitory appeared (as we know it to be) in comparison with the eternal of no account at all. I knew then that the only thing that matters when trouble is appointed is our attitude toward that trouble; and I turned from the telescope to meet the next assault with an entirely new peace. This that I must touch and handle and feel was nothing of real moment. A few days or months or years, and it would be forgotten utterly. But how I touched and handled it, how I felt and acted toward those who caused it – that belonged to the eternal order.

TO ACCEPT THE WILL OF GOD never leads to the miserable feeling that it is useless to strive any more. God . . . asks for something vivid and strong. He asks us to cooperate with him, actively willing what he wills, our only aim his glory. To accept in this sense is to come with all the desire of the mind unto the place which the Lord shall choose, and to minister in the name of the Lord our God *there* – not otherwise.

THOUGH THROUGH THESE MONTHS *acceptance* has been a word of liberty and victory and peace to me, it has never meant acquiescence in illness, as though ill health were from him who delights to deck his priests with health. But it did mean contentment with the unexplained. Neither Job nor Paul ever knew (so far as we know) why prayer for relief was answered as it was. But I think that they must stand in awe and joy, as they meet others in the heavenly country who were strengthened and comforted by their patience and valor, and the record of their Father's thoughts of peace toward them. Hardly a life that goes deep but has tragedy somewhere within it; what would such do without Job? And who could spare from his soul's hidden history the great words spoken to Saint Paul, "My grace is sufficient for thee, for my strength is made perfect in weakness" (2 Cor. 12:9)? Such words lead straight to a land where there is gold, and the gold of that land is good.

Gold – the word recalls Job's affirmation, "When he hath tried me I shall come forth as gold" (Job 23:10); and Saint Peter's "The trial of your faith, being much more precious than of gold that perisheth, though it be tried with fire" (1 Pet. 1:17); and the quiet word in Malachi, "He shall sit as a refiner and purifier of silver" (Mal. 3:3). . . .

This picture of the refiner is straight from Eastern life. The Eastern goldsmith sits on the floor by his crucible. For me, at least, it was not hard to know why the Heavenly Refiner had to sit so long. The heart knows its own dross. Blessed be the love that never wearies, never gives up hope that even in such poor metal he may at last see the reflection of his face.

"How do you know when it is purified?" we asked our village goldsmith.

"When I can see my face in it," he answered.

THERE ARE TIMES when something poignant brings home to us that we live in a suffering land. The mind faints before pain-smitten millions; and because the subject is so overwhelming, presently it does overwhelm, and crushes out even feeling. But just as where spiritual wrong is concerned, so it is here: lift one single suffering thing out of the mass, one small tormented child, and look at it, and the mind is numb no longer.

IT IS NEVER SAFE FOR A CONVERT, or for a child who is practically a convert, to be unhappy for long. Behind him or her is a darkness. Phantoms haunt that darkness, and memories, like hands, are ever pulling, pulling. . . . For eighteen months, in tension of spirit, we waited; but such a time is timeless; it might have been eighteen years. And we learned to accept the mystery of a delayed answer to our prayers, even to such an urgent prayer as this had been. . . . And in the end, not gradually as it had crept over her, but suddenly as at a word of command, the gloom passed. And that dear child, fully delivered, became our fellow soldier in the battles of the Lord.

The lesson that had been set us was the willing acceptance of daily, nightly perplexity and disappointment without explanation. In the Gospels such a matter was always dealt with instantly, and we had seen instant salvation and had read of the same in books. Here was delay. And we were not told why, and have not yet been told. We learned to accept the silence of our God.

CAN YOU FIND A PROMISE that if we follow the Lord Jesus Christ, life is going to be fairly easy? I do not think we shall find even one. But we shall find ever so many promises assuring us that however things are, we may count on strength to make us brave and peace to keep our hearts at rest.

I WANT YOU TO WELCOME the little difficult things, the tiny pricks and ruffles that are sure to come almost every day. For they give you a chance to say "No" to yourself, and by doing so you will become strong not only to do but also to endure.

Whatever happens, don't be sorry for yourselves. You know how our Lord met the tempting "Pity thyself" (Matt. 16:22). After all, what is anything we have to bear in comparison with what our Lord bore for us?

THERE IS A SECRET DISCIPLINE appointed for every man and woman whose life is lived for others. No one escapes that discipline, nor would wish to escape it; nor can any shelter another from it. And just as we have seen the bud of a flower close round the treasure within, folding its secret up, petal by petal, so we have seen the soul that is chosen to serve, fold round its secret and hold it fast and cover it from the eyes of man. The petals of the soul are silence.

It was so with Kohila when she saw some of her schoolfellows married and with dear children about them, and felt that for her that was not to be; for she knew and was sure that for her the other way was appointed; and he who had called her to that other way satisfied her heart.

DEUTERONOMY 2:3: "Ye have compassed this mountain long enough: turn you northward." It would take too long to tell what this word has said to me. I will only say it spoke about a mountain of thought round which I have walked rather often. It is time to stop compassing that mountain.

After settling that matter, I remembered one who for two whole years has been walking round a certain mountain of desire. When the desired thing was not given at the expected time, there was great disappointment. Perhaps the Lord is saying to that one and to others who are constantly praying about something personally desired, "Leave the matter to me: you have prayed enough about it. You have compassed that mountain long enough."

I know another who always seems to be walking round a mountain of rubble. Self and the feelings of self, doubts and questions, grumblings, little piled-up ingratitudes – what are these but rubble? Is it not very dull to keep on compassing so dull a mountain? Hear the heartening word of the Lord, "Ye have compassed this mountain long enough: turn you northward."

MORE THAN HALF THE TROUBLES that come to us come because of words. There is a question that has often helped me: "Wherefore hearest thou men's words?" (1 Sam. 24:9).

I suggest that next time you are afflicted by words you should let that quiet question do its work in your heart. No one yet did anything worth doing without finding, sooner or later, that words buzzed about him (or her) in a most distressing way. May the Lord help us to go on lovingly, peacefully, steadfastly. "My heart is fixed, O God, my heart is fixed: I will sing and give praise" (Ps. 57:7). One look up into the face of our Lord, and the thought of any hurting word melts like a little cloud in the blue of the sky above us.

THE SON SAID, "I am nothing."

His Father said, "Did I ever tell thee that thou wert something?"

The son said, "But I do not feel fit for this that is given to me to do."

His Father said, "Canst thou not trust me to make thee fit?"

The son said, "But I am not successful."

His Father said, "At the end of the day will my word be, 'Come, thou good and successful servant?' If only thou wilt walk humbly with thy God it will be, 'Come, thou good and faithful servant'" (Matt. 25:21).

The son said, "But I do not care for what I have to do."

His Father answered, "At last thou hast touched the root of the matter. Did thy Savior 'care for' Calvary?"

Then the Eternal Spirit opened to him those terrible scriptures which show Gethsemane and Calvary, till all his paltry "buts" were shriveled as withered leaves in the fire. And he saw him whom he followed as he set his face like a flint; and he was utterly confounded and ashamed.

O LORD, WHY? Why didst thou make flesh like a field threaded all over with roads and lanes where burning feet continually do pass? Men, women, children, beasts, birds, and some of the water-creatures – why, knowing what was to be, didst thou make them so? And the spirit of man, tuned like a delicate stringed instrument to the lightest touch, why, when it was to be smitten as by red-hot rods, didst thou make it so? Why build the house of life with every door set open to the devouring flame? . . .

What, then, is the answer? I do not know. I believe that it is one of the secret things of the Lord, which will not be opened to us till we see him who endured the cross, see the scars in his hands and feet and side, see him, our beloved, face to face. I believe that in that revelation of love, which is far past our understanding now, we shall "understand even as all along we have been understood" (1 Cor. 13:12).

And till then? What does a child do whose mother or father allows something to be done which it cannot understand? There is only one way of peace. It is the child's way. The loving child trusts. . . .

There is only one place where we can receive, not an answer to our question, but peace – that place is Calvary. An hour at the foot of the cross steadies the soul as nothing else can. "O Christ beloved, thy Calvary stills all our questions."

IT IS FOR GOD TO CHOOSE how he will heal. Our part is to cooperate, to set the forces of the will toward health, and to refuse to be dominated by the feeling of illness, depression, selfishness, weariness. If that be done, the prayer of faith is answered. The sick one is made sound so that he himself is well. (We are not our bodies.)

ONE DAY, DEEP IN THE FOREST, we came upon a rock in midstream scooped by the backwash of immemorial waters to a hollow like the palm of a man's hand. Over this rock fell a crystal sheet of water, and through that moving clearness we saw maidenhair fern growing in lovely profusion in the hollow of the hand. It was not the place where we should have planted a fern; at any moment it might have been tossed, a piteous, crumpled mass, down the shouting river – this is how it seemed to us. But it was safe. The falls flowed over it, not on it. And it was blessed. When the fern on the bank shriveled in heat, it was green, for it was watered all the year long by dust of spray. So does our wonderful God turn that which had seemed to be a perpetual threat to a perpetual benediction. Is there anything to fear with such a God?

Notes

Who Was Amy Carmichael?

This biographical sketch is based on *Amy Carmichael of Dohnavur,* by Frank Houghton; *A Chance to Die,* by Elisabeth Elliot; and Amy Carmichael's own works, particularly *Gold Cord.*

xv	However, on January 13	*A Chance to Die,* 52
	Thee must never say	*Kohila,* 112-13
xvi	As evening by evening	*Ponnammal,* 29
xvii	Haunted by flocks of noisy goats	*Gold Cord,* 39
	Framed between red roofs	*Lotus Buds,* 149
xviii	When we went back	*Overweights of Joy,* 287–88
	Could it be right to turn	*Gold Cord,* 40
ix	We let our feet be tied	*Gold Cord,* 41
	With the coming of each new child	*Gold Cord,* 35
	Sometimes we felt as though	*Gold Cord,* 23
xx	The care of young children	*Gold Cord,* 41
	To unite and fortify them	*Gold Cord,* 158
	Humbly imitated the manner	*Amy Carmichael of Dohnavur,* 217
	Times of vital silence	*Amy Carmichael of Dohnavur,* 37
xxi	Never forget that the human	*Kohila,* 64
	She ran to her bedroom	*Amy Carmichael of Dohnavur,* 89
	A pattern for the members	*Gold Cord,* 161–62
xxii	We were first shown	*Gold Cord,* 50
	One careful rule	*Gold Cord,* 50
	Learn to be a deep well	*Amy Carmichael of Dohnavur,* 38
xxiii	When the fellowship	*Windows,* 11
	When decisions have to be made	*Amy Carmichael of Dohnavur,* 258

Reading Amy Carmichael Today

Chapter 1. Nothing Kept Back

Chapter 2. Always a Soldier

Chapter 3. Prayer Hunger

Chapter 4. Your Chief Love and Friend

43	I think often we miss much	*Candles in the Dark,* 15
44	But when he was yet	*Windows,* 174
	We all know	*Edges of His Ways,* 177
45	God loves	*Gold by Moonlight,* 99
	Not in one sudden outpouring	*Kohila,* 119–120
46	Cast not away	*Gold by Moonlight,* 68–69
47	Feelings can be shaken	*Candles in the Dark,* 2
	But if we are defeated?	*Edges of His Ways,* 33
48	And he had in his right hand	*Edges of His Ways,* 12
	You often remind me	*Candles in the Dark,* 111
	Often our flash of haste	*Gold by Moonlight,* 112
49	There comes a time	*Gold by Moonlight,* 61
50	We have each our own	*Windows,* 176
51	On a rainy day in the forest	*Windows,* 176–77
52	We returned from that village	*The Widow of the Jewels,* 86
	Without him, lover of all lovers	*Gold Cord,* 63

Chapter 5. Forget Yourself in Serving Others

53	God gives love	*Candles in the Dark,* 110
	Stand by your fellowship	*Amy Carmichael of Dohnavur,* 351
	Some of you who are longing	*Candles in the Dark,* 4
54	Before the children came	*Gold Cord,* 76
	The rooms are Indian	*Gold Cord,* 76
55	When we were an itinerating band	*Lotus Buds,* 238–39
	We have found it possible	*Gold Cord,* 183–84
56	The Accals	*Lotus Buds,* 217–18

Chapter 6. Poetry of Childhood

Chapter 7. Embracing God's Will

Regarding the many Bible versions cited in her writings, Amy Carmichael wrote in 1932: "In case any are puzzled by the different translations from which I draw strength and help and delight, it is like this: In studying any object with the microscope we use different lenses and turn the mirror in various ways; each change brings out some new wonder and beauty. So it is for those who are not Greek or Hebrew scholars, and who use the work of scholars to open the meaning of the inexhaustible Word – the Bible is richer than any single version can fully show."

Bibliography

Carmichael, Amy. *Candles in the Dark: Letters of Amy Carmichael.* London: SPCK, 1981.

_____. *Edges of His Ways: Selections for Daily Reading from the Notes of Amy Carmichael.* London: SPCK, 1955.

_____. *Gold by Moonlight: Lessons for Walking Through Pain.* London: SPCK, 1940.

_____. *Gold Cord: The Story of a Fellowship.* London: SPCK, 1937.

_____. *His Thoughts Said . . . His Father Said. . . .* London: SPCK, 1940.

_____. *If.* London: SPCK, 1982.

_____. *Kohila: The Shaping of an Indian Nurse.* London: SPCK, 1956.

_____. *Lotus Buds.* London: Morgan and Scott, 1909.

_____. *Overweights of Joy.* London: Morgan and Scott, 1906.

_____. *Ploughed Under: The Story of a Little Lover.* London: SPCK, 1935.

_____. *Ponnammal: Her Story.* London: SPCK, 1939.

_____. *Rose from Briar.* London: SPCK, 1933.

_____. *Things as They Are: Mission Work in Southern India.* London: Morgan and Scott, 1903.

_____. *Though the Mountains Shake.* New York: Loizeaux Brothers, 1946.

_____. *Toward Jerusalem.* London: SPCK, 1936.

_____. *The Widow of the Jewels.* London: SPCK, 1930.

_____. *Windows.* London: SPCK, 1938.

Elliot, Elisabeth. *A Chance to Die: The Life and Legacy of Amy Carmichael.* Old Tappan, NJ: Fleming H. Revell, 1987.

Houghton, Frank. *Amy Carmichael of Dohnavur: The Story of a Lover and Her Beloved.* London: SPCK, 1953.

Plough Spiritual Guides

The Reckless Way of Love
Notes on Following Jesus
Dorothy Day

Love in the Void
Where God Finds Us
Simone Weil

The Prayer God Answers
Eberhard Arnold and Richard J. Foster

Why We Live in Community
Eberhard Arnold and Thomas Merton

The Two Ways
The Early Christian Vision of Discipleship
from the Shepherd of Hermas and the Didache
Introduction by Rowan Williams

The Scandal of Redemption
When God Liberates the Poor, Saves Sinners, and Heals Nations
Oscar Romero

Plough Publishing House
845-572-3455 ✦ info@plough.com
PO BOX 398, Walden, NY 12586, USA
Robertsbridge, East Sussex TN32 5DR, UK
4188 Gwydir Highway, Elsmore, NSW 2360, Australia
www.plough.com